Ella Koster
201-2279 McCallum Rd
Abbotsford BC V2S 6J1

CELEBRATE LIFE IN CANADA

D0981607

A Sword on the Land

Again the word of the Lord came unto me, saying, Son of man, speak to the children of thy people, and say unto them, When I bring the sword upon a land, if the people of the land take a man of their coasts, and set him for their watchman: If when he seeth the sword come upon the land, he blow the trumpet, and warn the people; Then whosoever heareth the sound of the trumpet, and taketh not warning; if the sword come, and take him away, his blood shall be upon his own head. He heard the sound of the trumpet, and took not warning; his blood shall be upon him. But he that taketh warning shall deliver his soul.

Ezekiel 33:1-4

A Sword on the Land

The Muslim World in
Bible Prophecy

by Bill Randles

ISBN 0-9646626-6-3

Acknowledgements

Extracts from the Authorized Version of the Bible (The King James Bible), the rights in which are vested in the Crown, are reproduced by permission of the Crown's patentee, Cambridge University Press.

Extracts from the NEW AMERICAN STANDARD BIBLE, © 1960, 1962, 1963, 1968, 1971, 1972, 1973, 1975, 1977, 1995, By the Lockman Foundation. Used by permission.

Second Publication: Lightning Source

First publication:
St. Matthew Publishing Ltd
1 Barnfield, Common Lane, Hemingford Abbots
Huntingdon PE28 9AX UK 01480 399098
Email: PF.SMP@dial.pipex.com www.stmatthewpublishing.co.uk

Table of Contents

To the elect lady whom I love in truth, the bride, the church which Jesus purchased in His own blood. Particularly, Believers in Grace Fellowship. You have supported me in my writing and ministry and I appreciate how God has used your faithfulness and Love to touch so many.

Foreword
Jacob Prasch

A sleeping church and a foolish world. Let us address the latter first. Bill Randles is one of those thinking authors who realize that the mainstream media spin the truth, and the politicians of all political parties invent the lies. Academic institutions lend a false credence to the demonstrable lies.

Perhaps the biggest of these obvious lies today is the insidious claim that Islam is a religion of peace and tolerance; a hideous proposition that no person of reasonable intelligence looking at the irrefutable evidence would believe. Yet, the biased media, godless governments, such as those in Washington and London, as well most anywhere else, and the left-leaning university establishment demand – and generally obtain – a compliant acceptance of a plain fallacy. These voices cannot point to a single Islamic country that gives Christians, or Jews, or women the same rights and freedom Moslems receive in Western countries, such as the USA, Britain & Europe, Australia, and Israel.

Absurdly, the same left-wing proponents of the feminist and homosexual & lesbian agendas conspicuously overlook the human rights record of women and homosexuals under Sharia and throughout the Moslem world in a level of hypocrisy that is difficult to rationally fathom.

Voltaire once defined history as "the lie everybody agrees upon." However, in today's world of unprincipled leaders like Cameron, Bush, Clinton, Blare, and Obama, and the editorialized reporting of events by CNN, the BBC, and the New York Times, and lowest-common-denominator popular entertainment like 'The View' and 'Oprah,' (or Barak Obama's personal favorite, 'the Pimp with a Limp'), the news has also now become "the lie that everyone agrees upon."

Bill Randles also recognizes a trend even more disturbing, however. It is not what transpires in the secular world or its corridors of power, but what is transpiring, or perhaps better phrased as, "failing to transpire," within what is

i

suppose to be the Evangelical church.

We are in an age of the apostasy that scripture warned would come prior to the return of Jesus. There are many aspects of this apostasy, but one key aspect that Bill Randles is aware of is the growing obliviousness of so much of the contemporary, supposedly Evangelical, church to eschatology and the fulfillment of prophecy. Rick Warren deceives the church in direct defiance of the Olivet Discourse instructions of Jesus to be alert for the signs He gave, including the Jews returning to Israel and Jerusalem in Luke 21:24, Matthew 23:39, and in Zechariah chapter 12. Yet as these much-predicted events unfold before our eyes, and the same nations at the center of events in scripture are at the center of global events today, Satan has moved to mislead and deceive the church through such false teachers as Rick Warren and supporter John Piper, who rejects the prophetic purposes of God for Israel and the Jews. Indeed, Warren urges Christians to avoid end-time prophecy as a diversion, and in his global peace plan, works to set the anti-Christ agenda to unite with worshippers of other gods (which Paul and Moses call demons), and other faiths, be it Islam, Hinduism, Buddhism or otherwise, in order to usher in global peace.

We also see a trend among professing Evangelicals, including Stephen Sizer, Gary Burge, and Colin Chapman, to turn their backs on the persecuted church in the Islamic countries, and rather single out Israel criticism and opposition when Israel is the one nation in the Middle East protecting the human rights and religious freedom of its Christian population.

Meanwhile, the popular media and corrupt Western politicians and academics spoon feed the public the obvious lie that Islam is a religion of peace and tolerance, demanding in the name of political correctness that they cannot point to a single Islamic nation that will grant Christians and Jews the same rights that Moslems are granted in the West; neither can they deny the staggering numbers of Moslems living in the West who openly admit their desire for Islamic Sharia over democracy.

God has a controversy with the Islamic Arab world and with Iran. In the books of Daniel, Isaiah. Jeremiah and in others we encounter the divine

ii

judgment that the Islamic world is going to encounter in retribution for Islam's persecution of Christians and hatred of Israel and the Jews.

An avalanche of divine destruction is coming to the Islamic world, and God has promised that He will raise His hand against these countries and their governments. As Bill Randles additionally recognizes, however, "Judgment Begins In The House of God, and if the Righteous are scarcely saved, what shall become of the ungodly and the sinner?"

You will profit by this timely book.

Introduction

I offer this book, *A Sword On The Land...The Muslim Nations In Prophecy*, out of a desire to interpret the handwriting on the wall for our times. Those who know the Bible understand the metaphor, but for those who don't, it comes from the book of Daniel, in the last days of the Babylonian Empire. The Babylonians were besieged by enemies, but they were so confident in their ability to prevail, they spent what proved to be their last evening as an empire in a drunken, raucous, licentious party! But the party was interrupted by a disturbing sight, for a hand appeared, writing on the wall of the royal party hall the cryptic words: *Mene, Mene, Tekel, Uppharsin*! Those at the party could see the hand writing, but couldn't interpret the meaning of the words.

I liken our current generation in the West to that final Babylonian party. We have become so proud of our technology and innovation that we have indulged in a long (post-World War II to present), riotous, cultural party, casting off our former religion, experimenting with drugs (legal and illegal), psychology, Eastern religions, atheism, and sexual immorality. Many modern people are oblivious to the manifold dangers we face and completely caught unaware of the ruin, temporal and spiritual, that looms before us.

But in our lifetime, a hand has written on our own wall, (9-11 for us Americans). A good many people now know there is something that portends woe; they know something isn't right in our societies, but they have no one to interpret it for them. What is the meaning of the sudden explosion of Muslim violence upon the world scene? What does the "Arab Spring" portend? What on earth is going on?

God is certainly working in all of these circumstances, but what is He saying?

What I am trying to do in this book is to answer some of these questions by drawing people's attention to the ancient prophecies, which are literally being fulfilled before our eyes.

My hope for my Christian brothers and sisters is that they be ready for the coming of the Lord. Also that they be equipped to witness to this generation, combining scripture with current events. People know that events are heading towards some kind of an apocalyptic climax and need to be shown the way of salvation before it is too late.

I also pray that this book gives some answers to any non-Christians who are wondering what is going on. I want you to see that God's Word is true. Ancient prophecies are being fulfilled to the letter in today's current events. Those who are shown these things may well be compelled to consider the rest of the Bible, seeing that it is indeed a supernatural book.

Finally, I want to reach out to any Muslims who happen upon this book. The same Hebrew prophets who predicted these occurrences in such accurate detail also pointed to the Messiah, the Savior of the World, the Lord Jesus Christ. They also prophesied centuries before His coming, how Jesus suffered, died for our sins, and rose again, as the token that He truly was sent from God to be our Savior! This same Jesus is coming again, to judge the world in righteousness, but whosoever "calls upon the name of the Lord shall be saved." Dear Muslim people, consider these prophecies and call upon the name of Jesus, for He is merciful and will abundantly forgive us of our sins.

If you are reading it, God is the one who put it in your reach, that you might see and consider that the Bible is unlike any other book, describing in detail, the end from the beginning, that you might believe and be saved. Finally, fulfilled prophecy is unique to the Bible; there is no other "holy book" of any other religion that can make this claim,

Remember the former things of old: for I am God, and there is none else; I am God, and there is none like me,

Declaring the end from the beginning, and from ancient times the things that are not yet done, saying, My counsel shall stand, and I will do all my pleasure: (Isaiah 46:9-10)

What we are seeing today, geopolitically, among the Muslim nations of the world is exactly what Bible prophets told us to expect centuries ago, in the times leading up to the final appearing of our Lord and Savior, Jesus Christ.

My method is simple: I examine the prophecies of Isaiah, Jeremiah, Joel Zechariah and others, but update the ancient names into the modern ones. The prophecies hold their relevance. For example, there is no longer a nation called "Edom," but there are many, many prophecies concerning the end times, yet unfulfilled, which concern Edom. These prophecies refer to the people who inhabit the present geographical location of Edom. So also for Ammon, Moab, Kedar, Dedan. This is the way I have approached these prophecies.

Others have done perhaps a better job of this. I know Arnold Fruchtenbaum has written articles on the *Arab States in Prophecy*, and Walid Shoebat wrote a book, *God's War On Terror*, which does this kind of work also. This is my own humble contribution to the body of literature on this subject.

I have not written to show that the Antichrist is Muslim, (I don't believe he is), but to highlight one huge part of much of Biblical prophecy and to prepare people for the coming of our Lord and Savior, Jesus Christ.

The premise for this little book is simple: update the names of the ancient peoples and regions in the prophecies of the Old and New Testament, and see how relevant these prophecies are to our modern day. I realize that many of the prophecies have been fulfilled already, in history, and in fact fulfilled prophecy is a confirmation that the Bible is the Word of God.

But the interpretation of Bible prophecy is a bit more complicated than prediction/fulfillment. Much of the prophecy of the Bible has a multiple and multilevel fulfillment, which intensifies as we come into the eschaton. Rather than a straight line between prediction to fulfillment, picture a corkscrew of repetitious fulfillment leading to the consummate fulfillment. For example, consider the prophecy of Daniel about the "abomination that makes desolate":

And he shall confirm the covenant with many for one week: and in the midst of the week he shall cause the sacrifice and the oblation to cease, and for the overspreading of abominations he shall make it desolate, even until the consummation, and that determined shall be poured upon the desolate. (Daniel 9:27)

Jesus alluded to this in Matthew 24, telling us to understand it, and to realize that when it happens, it should be a sign to us of His soon coming.

When ye therefore shall see the abomination of desolation, spoken of by Daniel the prophet, stand in the holy place, (whoso readeth, let him understand:) (Matthew 24:15)

The problem was that the "Abomination that makes desolate" had already happened, in the days of the Maccabees, more than a hundred years earlier. Daniel had predicted the sacrilege committed by Antiochus Epiphanes, who offered a pig on the Holy Altar of the Temple, but Jesus warned us to be on the alert for it!

There are some who say Jesus was warning us of 70 AD, and in part he was, but he used Daniel's prophecy as a reference. In 70 AD, the Temple was abominated again, as it was in 120 AD, (the Romans built a shrine to Jupiter on the Temple mount). The Temple Mount was further abominated by the erection of the "Dome of the Rock" and the "Al Aqsa Mosque," which also is an "abomination that makes desolate."

Finally, Paul warns of the same kind of sacrilege when he tells us of the Antichrist, and the ultimate "Abomination that makes desolate":

Let no man deceive you by any means: for that day shall not come, except there come a falling away first, and that man of sin be revealed, the son of perdition; Who opposeth and exalteth himself above all that is called God, or that is worshipped; so that he as God sitteth in the temple of God, shewing himself that he is God. (2 Thess 2:3-4)

There is a sense in which some prophecies occur over and over again. "Babylon the great is fallen, is fallen." Indeed it did, and it was recorded in Daniel 5 on the night of the "hand writing on the wall," but it happens over again. There is a sense in which Babylon falls, religiously, economically, and even geographically at the end of time. Economic Babylon must fall again (Revelation 18), so must religious Babylon (Revelation 17), as also political Babylon (Revelation 19). Though Babylon fell long ago, it must fall again in the end times to fulfill the prophecies.

We live in interesting times, for geographically, Babylon is here again (southern Iraq), as is Persia (Iran). Israel's traditional cousin enemies, Ammon, Moab and Edom are here (Jordan), so is Rome (the European Union). Syria has a role to play, especially Damascus, so do Dedan and Keder (Saudi Arabia), Sheba (Yemen), Libya, Egypt, Tyre and Sidon (southern Lebanon). Gomer and Togarmeh are back (Turkey), as is Cush (Somalia, Ethiopia).

There are others, but suffice it to say the ancient nations of the time of the prophets are back in the world's headlines. This is significant! God is so orchestrating things that all of these ancient entities are in the news constantly, and they cannot be ignored, even though people would love to.

Of course, much attention has been given, and rightly so, to the chief actor in the drama, who was not even a factor a mere 80 years ago: that is, Israel. The re-emergence of Israel on the international scene is the key reason people should sit up and take notice that the end of this age is at hand, and that this is not just a drama, but sober and shattering reality.

Jerusalem is in the news and is the topic of discussion of the world's deliberating bodies, such as the U.N., the European Union, Russia, and the United States. If any of the so-called "Quartet" could just deal with the problem of Israel, and especially of Jerusalem, they would be considered a hero. How does the world wash its hands of this pesky problem?

The reason it is such an intractable problem is because of the vehement opposition of the above-mentioned ancient biblical nations. These nations all have a unifying factor that they never had before, and they have leverage also that never existed before.

The unification factor is Islam: a violent, pagan religion for whom the mere existence of Israel as a Western, Jewish nation in the Middle East is an affront! All of the above nations hate Israel because of Islam.

The leverage factor is that in most of these nations, God has seen fit to put much of the lifeblood of the modern world in their power, i.e., pure and easily accessible crude oil. And the Arab nations especially are using this as leverage to promote Islam and attack Israel. These things will lead to the end of the age.

What I seek to do in this little book is give a modern framework for understanding the entities discussed in the prophecies. I know there are many who will accuse me of applying ancient and already fulfilled prophecies to modern situations. Judge for yourself; be a Berean.

As I have said, the prophecies of the Bible have multiple fulfillments in some cases. They apply to the immediate situation in which the prophet lived, obviously, else how could anyone judge the prophet as God commanded them to do? But they look further down into history, all the way to the end of the age.

True it is that "Babylon has fallen," but not in the dramatic obliteration that Isaiah and Jeremiah predicted it would, at least not yet. Damascus was indeed taken over, as predicted by the prophets, but it has not yet "ceased to be a city," as Isaiah predicted. There is much that is future about these prophecies.

I don't claim to be a Greek or Hebrew scholar – I am a pastor who is concerned that God's flock be awake and alert to the times, and an evangelist who would love to see God's people "interpreting the handwriting on the wall" for the many, many concerned people who know something is going on, but who don't quite know what it is.

On another note, I am not being in any way exhaustive in this study, for I hope others will take what I have gleaned from good men such as Arnold Fruchtenbaum, Jacob Prasch, Bob Westbrook and Walid Shoebat, and bypass my limited scholarship.

These are the last days.

You know what I find ironic about our times? When I became a Christian in the late 1970s, the evangelical world was gripped with an eschatological vision: Jesus was coming and we couldn't wait for the day! Every once in a great while, something would happen in the world scene that was so clearly prophetic, there would be a buzz surrounding it that would last for about six months. Just once or twice a year, but people would encourage each other on the strength of that event for the next six months or so.

But now, thirty years later, every single day the newspapers pour out events, which are clear fulfillments of prophecy, and yet for the most part, evangelicals don't even notice it. These are unprecedented times, wisdom is crying out in the streets, a great big hand is writing on this decadent culture's wall, but much of the church has been lulled into a profound slumber.

I dedicate this book to the reawakening of the Pentecostal and evangelical church, and to the multitudes out there who may not even be Christian, but like Rahab the harlot, they have a sneaking suspicion that something is desperately amiss! *Maranatha!*

Chapter 1 - The Arab World Unraveling

The earth is utterly broken down, the earth is clean dissolved, the earth is moved exceedingly. The earth shall reel to and fro like a drunkard, and shall be removed like a cottage; and the transgression thereof shall be heavy upon it; and it shall fall, and not rise again. And it shall come to pass in that day, that the LORD shall punish the host of the high ones that are on high, and the kings of the earth upon the earth. (Isaiah 24:9-11)

We are currently witnessing an unraveling of the already fragile modern order of the Arab world. Current Arab nations were formed by the victorious allies of World War I, France and Britain, after they had defeated the Ottoman Turks, who had sided with the Germans in the conflict. Diplomats pored over maps, border lines were drawn, sometimes by straightedge, and nations were mapped out, such as Saudi Arabia, Syria, Jordan, "Palestine," Iraq and Lebanon.

During the post-war period, North Africa and the Arab Middle East came under the rule of either the British or French mandates. The Arabs, chafing under the yoke of being ruled by the "Christian West," formed dissident groups, such as the Muslim Brotherhood, which nurtured the ideal of a return to Allah as the only way to reverse the current humiliation.

On a more secular note, the Arab world churned with a swirling political maelstrom of Arab versions of Communism, Socialism and, in the thirties, even Hitlerism. Eventually, a special kind of Arabic fascist party was formed and took rule in both Syria and Iraq, which was called the Ba'athist party.

After World War II, an exhausted Britain and France began to undertake a "colonial retreat," which ultimately led to Arab independence and national self-determination. Two parallel movements have since been brewing in the Arab world, one secular and the other religious: Pan-Arabism and Islamist fundamentalism.

The period of the late 1940s through the 1960s proved to be turbulent years through the Arab world. Algeria threw off the French in a bloody Islamist-inspired war for independence. Egypt experienced a military revolt, by which Gamal Nasser replaced the decadent King Farouk as the nation's leader. All over the Middle East, similar things were occurring during the 'de-colonialization' period.

The new Arab leaders were secular for the most part. They were Muslim in name, but knew enough to keep movements such as the Muslim Brotherhood suppressed and on the run. Any dissent at all was brutally crushed. In nations such as Egypt, the people were kept distracted from their misery by a constant barrage of state-run, media-based conspiracy theories, blaming all problems on either the Jews or the Western powers.

These Middle Eastern leaders feared fundamentalist Islam; after all, they had much bitter experience to guide them. Nasser's successor in Egypt, Anwar Sadat, was assassinated by his own troops, who had been infiltrated by agents of the Muslim Brotherhood. Mubarek, his successor, wasn't about to let that happen to him.

King Hussein of Jordan killed 20,000 supporters and members of the PLO (Palestine Liberation Organisation) in one month when they tried to foment a rebellion on his soil in 1970. In another brutal example, when the Muslim Brotherhood inspired an uprising against the rule of Syria's Hafez Al Assad in the city of Hama, Syria in February 1982, Assad wasted no time crushing the revolt, killing tens of thousands of Syrians and bulldozing much of the old portion of the city as an example to any other potential revolutionaries.

Saddam Hussein brutally suppressed all domestic Sunni and Shiite terrorist groups, as did the Shah of Iran. The Assads of Syria knew they had to be ready and willing to brutally crush any Islamist uprising without hesitation. The Saudis have been no less ruthless in their rule.

2

Through brutality, these leaders repeatedly have crushed the aspirations of groups like the Muslim Brotherhood, because they knew better than anyone who they were dealing with. Egypt jailed and tortured hundreds, if not thousands, of those who were inspired by the writing of Hassan Al Banna and Sayyid Qutb to wage a Jihad violently, politically or otherwise, in order to restore the Caliphate and bring the world under Sharia.

In May of 1948, an event occurred in the heart of the Middle East that galvanized the Arab world against a new common enemy. In fulfillment of the prophecies of the Bible and against all world expectations, the nation of Israel was reborn in one day.

"Who has heard such a thing? Who has seen such things? Can a land be born in one day? Can a nation be brought forth all at once? As soon as Zion travailed, she also brought forth her sons. (Isaiah 66:8)

From that moment to today, the Jews, who had also, according to the ancient prophecies of scripture, been scattered around the world, began to come back into the Holy land.

Hear the word of the Lord, O ye nations, and declare it in the isles afar off, and say, He that scattered Israel will gather him, and keep him, as a shepherd doth his flock. They shall come with weeping, and with supplications will I lead them: I will cause them to walk by the rivers of waters in a straight way, wherein they shall not stumble: for I am a father to Israel, and Ephraim is my firstborn.

Behold, I will bring them from the north country, and gather them from the coasts of the earth, and with them the blind and the lame, the woman with child and her that travaileth with child together: a great company shall return thither. (Jeremiah 31;8-10)

Within hours of the announcement, the combined armies of five Arab nations gathered with the openly stated intent to drive this infant nation of holocaust survivors into the sea. Armed only with the remnants of surplus, cast off rifles and a few armored personnel carriers, Israel resoundingly defeated the massed Arab foes.

This humiliation became known among the Arab people as Al Naqba, "The Calamity," and to this day, that day is marked in much of the Arab world by mourning and demonstrations.

Since that day, in four separate wars, the combined might of the Arab world, superior in arms, personnel, and resources, has been unable to accomplish its great boast to erase Israel, wipe it off of the map, and push it out of existence into the sea! This impotence has been a constant source of humiliation and an affront to the religion of Islam. It was after the 1973-1974 Yom Kippur War that the conviction began to become widespread in the Arab world that only by an Islamic revival, a return to fundamentalist Islam, could Israel ever be annihilated. This concept is the fuel that ignites our current crisis.

Since then, Saudi Arabia has spent its billions in oil revenue to propagate its own nefarious brand of Islam. The Saudi royal family are the custodians of the sect known as Wahhabism: a puritanical, violent, holier-than-thou but with hand grenades, version of the religion. Through its Saudi financed madrassas, Wahhabism is inciting mass hatred and murder among the poverty-stricken Muslim masses in Africa, Indonesia, Pakistan, and throughout the world.

The Saudis have made a domestic devil's bargain with the Islamists, as far as the Arabian Peninsula is concerned. The Royal family will bankroll madrassas, "charities," mosques, and terrorist groups anywhere in the world. They will arm and train them, to go anywhere, as long as the "Kingdom" is left alone. However, trouble is brewing in Saudi Arabia also, for example, all but one of the 9-11 hijackers were Saudis.

Up until recently, most of the leadership in the rest of the Arab world has been secular and has resisted Islamism in their respective lands. The terrorists hate with a passion these secular rulers of the Arab countries, and they also hate the debauched and hypocritical Saudis, perhaps even more than they hate America.

What we are seeing in the Arab world is the breakup of this devil's bargain. The popular uprisings are not the Middle Eastern version of the democratic revolution of Jefferson, Madison and Washington part two. They are instead the popularly approved removal of the restraining forces on something even more brutal than the Mubareks, Attaturks, Assads or the Shah of Iran. These leaders are falling to the forces of the Islamic revival.

Such brutal leaders held back something even more savage than themselves, for they have restrained true Islam. Yes, the postwar Arab leaders were brutal, utilitarian and self-serving; they did what they had to do to keep their restive populations distracted and subdued. They knew what they were dealing within Islam.

What we are seeing in the Arab world right now is the removal of those restraints, the release of the long pent-up pressure, the opening of the floodgates again to the true followers of Mohammed.

Don't be deceived by the preferred narrative of the "Facebook" revolution. According to the popular Western media version of events in Egypt and elsewhere, supposedly peace-loving, cell phone- and Facebook-using Egyptians yearning for democracy have just toppled a dictator in a virtually bloodless revolution, and now all is well. Indeed, a thirty-something Egyptian Facebook exec initially was one of the leaders of this movement, but he has been rejected by the current leaders of the revolution in Egypt.

When the masses gathered on Tahriri Square to celebrate the abdication of Mubarak, the Facebook exec was forced away from the podium. Instead, the dais was given to the formerly exiled but wildly celebrated Egyptian preacher, Yusuf Al Qadrawi, who called upon the Egyptians to not be content until prayer was offered to Allah on the Temple Mount in Jerusalem.

The real face of the current Arabic revolution was revealed in the brutalization of the Western journalists, particularly the female reporter brutalized by a mob, chanting "Jew, Jew, Jew," as they performed unspeakable indignities on her in a public street.

These demonstrators are people who have been fed a steady diet of anti-Western, anti-Jewish conspiracy theories, and whose

5

main complaint with Mubarak was that he suppressed fundamentalist Islam and honored a peace treaty with Israel.

It is becoming increasingly evident, that the True and Living God, the Father of our Lord Jesus Christ, the Messiah, is uncorking the corks; He is releasing the forces that will culminate in Jerusalem for the last battle before the Millennium.

Keep reading, because this gets intense!

Chapter 2 – Sons of Ishmael

Looking at recent events in the Arab world, we see Tunisia, Egypt, Libya, Yemen, Jordan, Saudi Arabia, Dubai and others being shaken by massive, violent, popular demonstrations. Governments are falling, factions are being emboldened, and as in the late 1980s in the case of those Eastern European Soviet ruled nations, the fear of brutal leaders is dissolving.

There are two things these Middle Eastern nations have in common: they are Arabic and they are majority Muslim, in the midst of a revival of fundamentalist Islam. That is why the so-called "democratic" aspect of these upheavals is meaningless. As we have seen recently in Egypt, Islamist candidates will win popular elections in those nations, for those who live there believe that their current governments haven't been sufficiently Islamic.

This underscores the fact that there is a profound spiritual dimension to these events. We must look to the Word of God to see these upheavals from a God-centered perspective. God has much to say about the Arab people, for the prophets of the Bible foretold in great detail the origin and destiny of the Arab people.

There is a mixture of hope and gloom in the prophetic scenario. The sons of Abraham, Ishmael and of Esau play a prominent role in the Last Days scenario: some are slated to survive and be blessed of God, and others are headed for total destruction, even into the thousand year reign of Christ.

We must start in Genesis, in the story of the patriarch, Abraham. God promised him that He would make him "the father of a multitude of nations," and that of his seed, every family on earth would be blessed.

And I will make of thee a great nation, and I will bless thee, and make thy name great; and thou shalt be a blessing: And I will bless them that bless thee, and curse him that curseth thee: and in

7

thee shall all families of the earth be blessed. (Genesis 12:2-3)

The challenge of believing this promise was that Abraham's wife was barren and the couple were in their seventies. When the God of the Bible wants to create a new nation to be his witnesses on the earth, He doesn't select a young virile couple in their twenties. He instead chooses an old barren couple, "as good as dead," so that in their fruitfulness, He alone gets the glory! God gives life to the dead and calls those things that are not, as though they were.

But Abraham and Sarai began to doubt the promise after many fruitless years. They began to reason as to how this promise could be fulfilled, eventually coming up with what seemed to be a legitimate way to achieve the promise. Abraham had acquired a handmaiden named Hagar from the land of Egypt. She was young and fertile, and it was considered legal according to the laws of the land in those days to have a child by one's handmaid, as an heir.

At Sarai's bidding, Abraham slept with Hagar and she conceived. During her pregnancy, she grew haughty towards Sarai. This caused a lot of strife in the home, for Sarai dealt harshly in turn with Hagar.

And Sarai Abram's wife took Hagar her maid the Egyptian, after Abram had dwelt ten years in the land of Canaan, and gave her to her husband Abram to be his wife. And he went in unto Hagar, and she conceived: and when she saw that she had conceived, her mistress was despised in her eyes. And Sarai said unto Abram, My wrong be upon thee: I have given my maid into thy bosom; and when she saw that she had conceived, I was despised in her eyes: the LORD judge between me and thee. But Abram said unto Sarai, Behold, thy maid is in thine hand; do to her as it pleaseth thee. And when Sarai dealt hardly with her, she fled from her face. (Genesis 16:3-6)

Late in her pregnancy, the harsh treatment became so unbearable for Hagar that she fled Abraham's home out into the harsh wilderness. It was there in the howling wasteland that Hagar encountered an angel, who named the yet unborn child Ishmael, i.e.,

"God has heard," and sent Hagar back to Abraham's camp to bear Abraham's first-born son.

That son, Ishmael, is the father of the Arab people. So significant is Ishmael that, like Jesus, Samson, and John the Baptist, he too was named by an angel before he was even born.

And the angel of the LORD said unto her, Behold, thou art with child and shalt bear a son, and shalt call his name Ishmael; because the LORD hath heard thy affliction. And he will be a wild man; his hand will be against every man, and every man's hand against him; and he shall dwell in the presence of all his brethren. (Genesis 16:11-12)

The character of the Arab people is here prophetically described, in the first book of the Bible;

• **The divinely assigned name, Ishmael** – means either "God hears" or "He will hear God." Not all Arabs are the direct physical descendants of Ishmael, but through Islam, they are in spiritual affinity with Ishmael's disenfranchisement from Abraham.

• **A Wild Ass of a man** – The literal rendering of KJV's "Wild man." This is not meant to be taken as an insult, for to a desert-dwelling people, the wild ass represents toughness, virility, fierce independence, and unbrokenness: all of the qualities one would require to survive in a harsh and unforgiving environment.

• *His hand will be against every man and every man's against him* – Ishmael would be warlike, he would not submit to others who try to dominate him, and he would seek to dominate others.

• *He will dwell in the presence of his brothers* – This is the prediction that Ishmael would not only be at war with all other nations, but that he would be unable to have peace even with his own brothers. This passage can be interpreted as, "He will dwell in the face of his brothers."

• *Arab would be at war with Arab.* To this day, the prophecy holds true. Arabs, when not fighting outsiders, fight each other. "An enemy of my

9

enemy is my friend, and a friend of my enemy is my enemy," goes an Arab proverb. He shall ever live '*in the face of his brothers.*'

• **The Arabs would be a powerful, populous people** – The Angel who appeared to Hagar in the desert, prophesying Ishmael's birth, also predicted that the Ishmaelites would be an exceedingly numerous people.

And the angel of the LORD said unto her, I will multiply thy seed exceedingly, that it shall not be numbered for multitude. (Genesis 16:10)

History has proven this prophecy to be true: the Arabs are the independent, fierce, unbroken survivors that the angel said they would be. They have also multiplied into a great nation; there are currently hundreds of millions of Arabs; there are 22 Arab nations in the Middle East and North Africa; and through Islam, Arab culture is predominant in 57 nations of the world.

But it is also a truism that the Muslims/Arabs have an inability to live in peace. Contrary to contemporary "wisdom," there is no place on earth where Islam has ever wrought any kind of peace, other than the peace of the dead! When the Arabs are not at war with the rest of the world, they are fighting among themselves. Arab against Arab, and Muslim against Muslim is the rule and not the exception.

Finally, the Muslim/Arabs have a fierce, unyielding hatred for their younger brother, Isaac (i.e., Israel).

The Muslim narrative of how the Arabs came to be and who exactly the promised one of God would be, takes the perspective of Ishmael. There is a Muslim feast called Eid Al Adha, which celebrates the sacrifice of Ishmael, for Islam claims Ishmael to be the chosen one. (I recently heard that the etymology of the word 'Saracen' means 'emptied of Sara,' from Hagar's complaint "Sara has sent us away empty"). I do not know if this is true, but it is an interesting theory.

Islam is definitely of a spiritual affinity with Ishmael.

Ishmael was thirteen years old, the "seed of Abraham" and the firstborn, and heir to Abraham's blessing, when the promise of God was fulfilled in truth, for Sarah did conceive and gave birth to Isaac, whose name means laughter, because his mother laughed at the prospect of conceiving him.

Ishmael and his mother Hagar teased and tormented little Isaac to the point that Abraham was instructed by God to send Ishmael and his mother out of the house! The false heir had to make way for the true heir to the promise of God.

It is this disenfranchisement that is the source of the utter hatred and complete malice the Arab Muslim world harbors towards Israel. Islam nurtures the original grievance of Ishmael and Hagar, his equally disenfranchised mother.

The scripture calls this hatred "the perpetual hatred," and predicts that this hatred of Ishmael for Isaac, and of Esau for Jacob, will be the catalyst for the final judgments to come down upon the whole world.

*Because thou hast had a **perpetual hatred,** and hast shed the blood of the children of Israel by the force of the sword in the time of their calamity, in the time that their iniquity had an end: Therefore, as I live, saith the Lord GOD, I will prepare thee unto blood, and blood shall pursue thee: sith thou hast not hated blood, even blood shall pursue thee.* (Ezekiel 35:5-6)

We will look next at another development in the formation of the Arab people, also recorded in Genesis, and pertaining to the future events unfolding now, in the prophesy concerning Esau.

Chapter 3 – In the Character of Esau

Obviously, Islam isn't mentioned by name in Bible prophecy, for it emerged in the 7th century, long after the Biblical canon was completed. But the Bible prophets are by no means silent about the followers of the vast, radical, monotheistic world religion that has since presented itself as the chief rival and alternative to the Judeo-Christian world.

From the beginning of the Word of God, in Genesis we see the origins of the Isaac/Ishmael and Jacob/Esau conflicts, which are currently being played out on the world stage. Islam's character and fate is foretold in the biblical record, in the stories of Ishmael and Esau and in the prophecies that foretell the future of those Arab, Turkish, African and Persian lands that have embraced Islam.

Esau is a figure in Biblical history who is of great importance in understanding what the Hebrew prophets have to say about the fate of the Arab Muslim world. He is a son of Isaac, the twin of Jacob, and nephew and son-in-law of Ishmael. Esau's remaining physical and spiritual descendants have a large role in the Last Days scenario.

We have already stated how Islam identifies with the grievance of Ishmael and has nourished the "everlasting hatred" of Isaac and Jacob as a result of it. Even so does Islam identify with the disenfranchisement of Esau, envying the Jews whom they see as interlopers upon their inheritance. It is comforting to know that all of these things were predicted, even before Jacob and his twin, Esau (the firstborn of Isaac and Rebekah), were born.

Rebekah his wife conceived. And the children struggled together within her; and she said, If it be so, why am I thus? And she went to enquire of the LORD. And the LORD said unto her, Two nations are in thy womb, and two manner of people shall be separated from thy bowels; and the one people shall be stronger than the other people; and the elder shall serve the younger. (Genesis 25:21-23)

The story of Isaac's struggling twins, Jacob and Esau, foreshadows the very events that the world is trembling and shaking over unto this day. The twins' fight is worldwide now; nations and peoples are having to take sides in the conflict. Neutrality is proving to be impossible. The Judeo-Christian world, and the Islamic and post-Christian world cannot truly coexist.

Consider the details of the prophecy at the birth of these two:

• **Esau and Jacob would be two nations** – Isaac's barren wife conceived twins, in answer to prayer. But the pregnancy was difficult, for there was much movement in the womb. The twins were literally wrestling within her. When she inquired of the Lord, this is the Word that came unto her:

"Two nations are in thy womb, and two manner of people shall be separated from thy bowels; and the one people shall be stronger than the other people; and the elder shall serve the younger."

• **Esau was the firstborn** – The Bible tells us that even when coming out of the womb, these two brothers wrestled for pre-eminence. Esau was born first. Traditionally the firstborn is given the birthright, the family leadership, double share of the inheritance, and the spiritual headship of the family. Certainly Isaac, the boy's father and heir of the promise, preferred Esau, but God chose Jacob.

• **One people would be stronger than the other** – He doesn't specify which, but ever would it be that one would be stronger than the other. History bears this out, for at times Israel prevailed over the surrounding Edomite/Ishmaelite people, and at other times was subdued by them.

• **The Elder shall serve the younger** – This would be a hard pill to swallow, for it goes against man's order. But God chose Jacob over Esau to be the repository of Abraham's blessing. The "seed of the woman" would come through Jacob, not Esau.

13

According to the prophecy given Rebecca, Esau and his seed would have to serve Jacob, whom God elected. The fate of Esau would be linked to whether or not he accepts Jacob's God and 'the seed of the woman' who would come through the line of Jacob. Obviously, carnal Esau bristled at that, as do all of those in spiritual affinity with Esau to this day.

On the other hand, millions of the seed of Ishmael and Esau have come under the covering of the God of Jacob, believing in the Messiah who came through Jacob and Judah. There are and have been untold millions of Arab Christians through the centuries, many concentrating in the Middle East. By clinging to Jacob's God, Esau would be saved.

• **Esau shall hate Jacob, envying him for his birthright** – First, Esau "sold" his birthright to his brother, Jacob, for a bowl of porridge. He then complained to everyone who would hear that Jacob tricked him out of it! The spiritual and physical descendants of Esau hate Jacob (Israel) to this day, swearing they have been cheated by him out of their 'birthright,' the land.

In reality, it was neither the machinations of Jacob or Esau, but the election of God himself, which conferred upon Jacob the birthright and the promise and blessing of Abraham.

Isaac blessed Jacob in the place of Esau, whom he intended to bless. He blessed him in spite of Esau's faithlessness (he married two Hittite women, over his parents' objection) and profanity (he counted the birthright for nothing). Isaac was determined to confer upon Esau the blessing of the firstborn. He had a great natural affection for his virile, accomplished son.

But God's election is all that really counts.

When the time came for the passing on of the patriarchal blessing, and Isaac had sent his favorite son, Esau, out for venison to cook and eat for the occasion, Rebecca and Jacob sprang into action, putting Jacob in the place of Esau in an elaborate deception, disguising Jacob as Esau.

And his father Isaac said unto him, Come near now, and kiss me, my son. And he came near, and kissed him: and he smelled the smell of his raiment, and blessed him, and said, See, the smell of my son is as the smell of a field which the LORD hath blessed: Therefore God give thee of the dew of heaven, and the fatness of the earth, and plenty of corn and wine: Let people serve thee, and nations bow down to thee: be lord over thy brethren, and let thy mother's sons bow down to thee: cursed be every one that curseth thee, and blessed be he that blesseth thee. (Genesis 27:26-29)

The blessing of Abraham, which had passed on down unto Isaac, was now passed to Jacob, the second-born twin. True, Isaac prophesied to Jacob wrongly, thinking he was conferring the blessing upon Esau, but God was working in the situation his own sovereign plan of election. Jacob was chosen by God; Esau, only by Isaac. God's good hand had overruled Isaac's carnal preference.

When Esau came in from hunting to prepare the venison his aged father loved, Isaac discovered the ruse that had been laid upon him,

And it came to pass, as soon as Isaac had made an end of blessing Jacob, and Jacob was yet scarce gone out from the presence of Isaac his father, that Esau his brother came in from his hunting. And he also had made savoury meat, and brought it unto his father, and said unto his father, Let my father arise, and eat of his son's venison, that thy soul may bless me. And Isaac his father said unto him, Who art thou? And he said, I am thy son, thy firstborn Esau. And Isaac trembled very exceedingly, and said, Who? where is he that hath taken venison, and brought it me, and I have eaten of all before thou camest, and have blessed him? **yea, and he shall be blessed.** (Genesis 27:30-33)

Notice Isaac's faith in the fact that he realized that the Blessing conferred upon Jacob was valid, God ordained the blessing, and it couldn't be reversed! *"...He shall be blessed."* This is why the book of Hebrews in the New Testament sums up this story in this fashion: *By faith Isaac blessed Jacob and Esau concerning things to come.* (Hebrews 11:20)

Esau's reaction was a vow to murder his brother at the earliest opportunity.

What we are seeing in the awakening of the Arab/Muslim world is the continuation of what started in that troubled pregnancy of Rebecca: Esau still wrestles with his brother, Jacob. He still accuses him of trickery, theft, treachery and usurpation. The conflict ceases only after the whole earth is embroiled in the struggle, and God Himself intervenes.

But Jacob did grant Esau a 'blessing' in response to his tearful entreaties, *And Esau said unto his father, Hast thou but one blessing, my father? bless me, even me also, O my father. And Esau lifted up his voice, and wept. And Isaac his father answered and said unto him, Behold, thy dwelling shall be the fatness of the earth, and of the dew of heaven from above; And by thy sword shalt thou live, and shalt serve thy brother; and it shall come to pass when thou shalt have the dominion, that thou shalt break his yoke from off thy neck.* (Genesis 27:38-41)

• **Behold your dwelling shall be the fatness of the earth** – Sounds good in the King James version, but what this literally says is you will dwell **away** from the fatness of the earth, and **away** from the dew of the heavens..,

Here from the New American Standard bible:

Behold, away from the fertility of the earth shall be your dwelling, and away from the dew of heaven from above.

Esau, or Edom, would dwell in a harsh, arid, brown environment. Geographical Edom is in the area around the Dead Sea and into southern Jordan, a dry, parched wilderness. Spiritual Edom, the Arab/Moslem world, is also parched. North Africa and the Middle East appear, even from space, to be brown as opposed to the lush green of the rest of Africa. The Arabian Peninsula is an arid place.

• **You shall live by your sword** - Edomites were a fierce, warlike tribe, ever at war with their neighbors and with each other. Modern Islamic terrorists make the boast often that, "We will prevail over the West, because we love death, and they love life!"

16

Esau would ever live by the sword; therefore, Esau would ever die also by the sword. According to the world's one billion Muslims, Mohammed, the best man who ever lived, lived by the sword as a pirate, raider, and terrorist. A true son of Edom.

• *And you shall serve your brother* – But for all of the exaltation of the sword, Esau must serve Jacob. We know that King David put the Edomites into subjection, by military conquest and cultural superiority.

But in another, better way, many of the descendants of Esau have served Jacob. There are millions of Arab Christians, sons of Ishmael, and of Esau, Moab, and Ammon, who have come to believe in the Gospel of the Jewish Messiah, and to worship the God of Jacob. Remember that in the earliest years of church history, all of the Middle East and North Africa was entirely Christian.

• **But when you shall become restless, you shall break his yoke off of your neck** – This also is from the New American Standard Bible, *"But it shall come about when you become restless, that you will break his yoke from your neck."*

The prediction is that in later times, Esau would become restless and break the yoke that joined Jacob and Esau off of his neck. History has borne that out in part, by the expansion of Islam in what was once a Christian Middle East. They have replaced for themselves an easy yoke with a heavy and intolerable one, Islam.

This is what we are seeing in the Arab world: a restless Esau, throwing off the yoke of any subservience to the Judeo-Christian world, and asserting once again the wild, violent, independent spirit of Esau.

Esau is a spiritual archetype of the Arab Muslim world, which has carried on the ancient grievance over the birthright. They hate Israel with a passion and would wipe her out if given the chance. This hatred will lead the whole world into "the time of Jacob's (greatest) trouble" and Israel's true night of wrestling first and then clinging to her God until the dawn.

Chapter 4 – The Names of the Arab Nations

We have been looking at the considerable attention the Word of God gives to the origin and fate of the Arab people. Genesis, the foundational book of the Holy Bible, contains history and prophecies of both Ishmael and of Esau, their character and descendants' fate to the end days.

In the rest of scripture, there is also great interest in the Arabs and their progeny. These children of Abraham are major players in the drama that is the end of the world. The Hebrew prophets speak almost as much about the fate of the Arab nations as they do the Jewish state.

As I said in the introduction, the key is to juxtapose the modern names for the people and regions over the ancient ones.

• **Edom** – Edom is a major figure in end-times Bible prophecy. Edom is another name for Esau, who we looked at in the last chapter, the twin brother of Jacob. God assigned Esau the area of southern Jordan around Mt. Seir, which is why Edom is sometimes referred to as Mt. Seir, such as in Ezekiel 35.

Son of man, set thy face against Mount Seir, and prophesy against it, And say unto it, Thus saith the Lord GOD; Behold, O Mount Seir, I am against thee, and I will stretch out mine hand against thee, and I will make thee most desolate. (Ezekiel 35:2-3)

There are several ways to designate the Edomite people: the political Kingdom of Edom is long gone, but the geographic region is well known, and of course there is the spiritual identity of those who have taken up Esau's ancient hatred of the Jews.

The Edomite Kingdom was defeated by David and Saul and made subject to Judah for centuries as a vassal state. They would play a role in the destruction of the temple by Nebuchadnessar II, rising up against their former rulers, cutting off escape routes and openly gloating in the destruction of the Jewish people.

Eventually, they intermarried with the Ishmaelites, Midianites, and Moabites, and comprise much of the Middle Eastern Arabs. Geographically, the Edomites are the Arabs of southern Jordan. Spiritually, the Edomites are the Muslim Arabs who hate Israel, boast in inhabiting the Holy land, and have possessed the temple mount. Edomites rejoiced in the horrors that befell the Jews in 70 AD and 120 AD, cutting off any escape routes the Jews would have used, and collaborating with the Roman enslavers of Israel.

Centuries later and in the same character, the Middle Eastern Muslim Arabs cooperated in the Nazi holocaust, rioted and performed pogroms in order to block the British from receiving any Jewish refugees fleeing from the Holocaust into the Holy Land, under British rule.

The prophet Obadiah proclaims the indictment against Edom in his short prophecy:

*For thy violence against thy brother Jacob shame shall cover thee, and thou shalt be cut off for ever. In the day that thou stoodest on the other side, in the day that the strangers carried away captive his forces, and foreigners entered into his gates, and cast lots upon Jerusalem, even thou wast as one of them. But thou shouldest not have looked on the day of thy brother in the day that he became a stranger; neither shouldest **thou have rejoiced over the children of Judah** in the day of their destruction; neither shouldest **thou have spoken proudly** in the day of distress. Thou shouldest not have **entered into the gate of my people** in the day of their calamity; yea, thou shouldest not have looked on their affliction in the day of their calamity, nor have laid hands on their substance in the day of their calamity; Neither shouldest **thou have stood in the crossway, to cut off those of his that did escape;** neither shouldest thou have delivered up those of his that did remain in the day of distress.* (Obadiah 10-14)

• **The Philistines** – The Philistines were not Arabs; they were Greeks or Phoenicians and were eventually wiped out by Israel. But there are a modern Arab people who have taken for themselves the name of the Philistines, i.e., the 'Palestinians.' It is they who have been granted by the world community the Gaza coastal area, which was originally granted to the tribe of Judah as part of his inheritance, but came under the dominion of the five Philistine cities.

I speak of the mixed Arabs who either inhabited or who immigrated into the Holy Land shortly before and ever since the 1948 rebirth of the Jewish state. For the most part, they are Muslim, and have been at war with Israel from her start. They took upon themselves the identity "Palestinians" in 1967 that they might gain legitimacy for the establishment of their state.

God has something to say to Palestinians, i.e., Philistines, regarding the end times:

Thus saith the Lord GOD; Because the Philistines have dealt by revenge, and have taken vengeance with a despiteful heart, to destroy it for the old hatred; Therefore thus saith the Lord GOD; Behold, I will stretch out mine hand upon the Philistines, and I will cut off the Cherethims, and destroy the remnant of the sea coast. And I will execute great vengeance upon them with furious rebukes; and they shall know that I am the LORD, when I shall lay my vengeance upon them. (Ezekiel 25:15-17)

In Biblical times, there were five Philistine cities: Ekron, Gath (the city of Goliath), Askelon, Ashdod with Gaza being the most prominent. Gaza is today, of course, the coastal region from which Jews were expelled in 2005, and where the terrorist entity Hamas has since seized control.

• **Moab and Ammon** – These are the names of Lot's sons, who were born of incest after he fled Sodom and Gommorah. Geographically, Ammon and Moab are the inhabitants of central and northern Jordan. The capital of Jordan is called Amman.

The Ammonites and Moabites were bitter resisters of Israel. When Israel made her exodus, God told her not to molest them or

20

take their land, and to pay for anything they took on their way through Moabite land. But the Moabites feared them nonetheless, and abused them, as the story of Balak and Balaam attests.

• **Lebanon** – Israel's northern neighbor, features in several prophecies of the end. Lebanon was once considered the only Christian country in the Middle East. When the 1967 six-day war broke out, it set in motion events that would considerably alter the makeup of this country.

Terrorists fled into Lebanon from Israel and Jordan, setting up enclaves in the south from which to launch attacks on northern Israeli towns. The mayhem they brought to the nation led to a bloody civil war in the 1970s, pitting Lebanese militias composed of Christians (Maronite, Philangists *et al.*) and various strains of Muslim Jihadists (PLO, Hezbullah, Salafists), as well as the Lebanese army.

As in all civil wars, there have been atrocities on both sides. Philangist militias massacred hundreds of Palestinian refugees in the Sabra and Shatila camps, supported by the Israeli defense forces. The PLO and mixed groups of foreign Muslim fighters overran Christian towns, such as Damour, slaughtering hundreds of men, women and children without mercy.

The nation of Syria took advantage of Lebanon's weakened state, arming the Muslim rebels and eventually invading Lebanon, occupying much of it, and has controlled it to this day, arming Hezbullah, controlling elections and even assassinating popular elected leaders. The U.N. and even the United States shed much blood trying to keep the warring factions from slaughtering each other; for example, this was the setting for the 1983 Marine Corps barracks' bombing.

In 1982, Israel invaded Lebanon after repeated terror attacks upon her cities, eventually cornering Yasser Arafat and the PLO in Beirut, only to have to stand down, allowing the U.N. to give Arafat and his terrorist army safe passage to Tunisia rather than the extermination that he and the terrorist apparatus of the PLO faced by the surrounding IDF.

Israel occupied southern Lebanon for 28 years, until domestic pressure forced them to withdraw in the year 2000. The credit for this withdrawal was given by the Muslim world to Hezbullah, the Shiite "party of Allah," and is considered to be the first modern victory of Islam over Israel.

The prophets speak much indeed of Lebanon regarding the last days, but specifically "**Tyre and Sidon**." That is, the region of southern Lebanon currently dominated by Hezbollah. Its terrorist leaders have been raining rockets on Israeli cities with seeming impunity as of late.

"Now what have you against me, Tyre and Sidon and all you regions of Philistia? Are you repaying me for something I have done? If you are paying me back, I will swiftly and speedily return on your own heads what you have done. For you took my silver and my gold and carried off my finest treasures to your temples. You sold the people of Judah and Jerusalem to the Greeks, that you might send them far from their homeland. (Joel 3:3-4)

• **Syria** – The modern nation of Syria is about one half of the Biblical Assyrian Empire. The other half would be roughly the modern country of Iraq. Usually the area we refer to as Syria is referred to by the name of its major city, Damascus. There are 67 mentions of Damascus in the word of God.

Thus says the LORD: "For three transgressions of Damascus, and for four, I will not turn away its punishment, Because they have threshed Gilead with implements of iron. But I will send a fire into the house of Hazael, Which shall devour the palaces of Ben-Hadad. I will also break the gate bar of Damascus, and cut off the inhabitant from the Valley of Aven, and the one who holds the scepter from Beth Eden. The people of Syria shall go captive to Kir," Says the LORD. (Amos 1:3-5)

• **Iraq** – is the modern name for roughly the eastern half of the Assyrian Empire. In the Bible it is referred to as Assyria, Babylon, or as the Land of the Chaldees.

• **Saudi Arabia** – The Kingdom of Saudi Arabia is of recent origin; it came about as a result of the cooperation that the Saud family gave the British in World War I and has only been in existence since 1932.

Biblically, the region is referred to as Dedan, Sheba, Midian and Kedar. Dedan and Sheba were sons of Abraham through Keturah, and Kedar was a son of Ishmael.

• **North Africa** – consisting of Egypt, Libya, Algeria, Tunisia, Morocco and Ethiopia, is a region that is in tumult as Islamists seek to hijack popular movements for democracy, which have toppled several governments. The Biblical names for the regions are Egypt, Ethiopia, Cush, Put, Libya, and Cyrene.

Some of the non-Arab nations featured in Bible prophecy are **Iran**, which is called Persia, or Elam; **Turkey**, which is called Gomer, Togarmah, and Yavan, or Greece. Remember that Turkey was the Greek mainland and that many of the books of the New Testament were written to Greek churches in what is now called Turkey.

The unifying feature of all of these nations is Islam. It is Islam that unites these nations in a common, visceral hatred of the West. It is also Islam that is currently causing these people to churn and roil in revolutions, throwing off the secular dictators who had tried to keep them by force in the modern world.

Chapter 5 – Egypt's Fate

Egypt is a very significant player in the drama that is the end-times scenario, according to the prophets of the Bible. Egypt has recently been in the forefront of the world news as a result of the popular overthrow of the thirty-year Mubarak government and the election of a candidate put forth by the Muslim Brotherhood.

Many around the world have high hopes for Egypt, believing that good can come out of the Egyptian "democratic" revolution, but with subsequent events, those hopes of an "Arab Spring" are fast fading. Egypt is already taking its new-found "freedom" as an opportunity to persecute its own indigenous Christians, the Copts. Within weeks of Mubarak's downfall, disturbing accounts have surfaced of church burnings, anti-Christian riots, murders, shootings, and a video of the Egyptian army assaulting a monastery, shooting at unarmed monks and destroying an abbey with armored personnel carriers.

Those who undermined and unseated Mubarak have also taken the opportunity to publicly renounce the thirty-year peace treaty with Israel and to clamor for war against the Jews. It's time to look closely at the prophecies relating to Egypt. Ironically, the scriptures tell us that Egypt indeed does have a bright future, but not as an outcome of a democratic revolution. The revolution that toppled Mubarak is already disintegrating into an open Muslim persecution against Coptic Christians, and calls for Israel to be annihilated in the name of Islam.

Amazingly, in the midst of the toppling of the Mubarak government, the foreign ministry of Egypt successfully brokered an agreement between bitter rivals, Fatah and Hamas, which allows them to form a unity government in the so-called "Palestinian Authority."

This, in effect, legitimizes Hamas, an unrepentant anti-Israel terror group dedicated to the destruction of Israel, as a valid partner that Israel must now negotiate with for "peace."

Because of God's promise to *"Bless those who bless you and curse those who curse you (Israel),"* Egypt is going to undergo a harsh night of tribulation before the breaking of the dawn, according to Isaiah and Ezekiel:

In that day shall Egypt be like unto women: and it shall be afraid and fear because of the shaking of the hand of the LORD of hosts, which he shaketh over it. And the land of Judah shall be a terror unto Egypt, every one that maketh mention thereof shall be afraid in himself, because of the counsel of the LORD of hosts, which he hath determined against it. (Isaiah 19:16-17)

Egypt has been seized by a mortal fear, particularly of the Jews, and God himself is in that fear. Keep in mind that Egypt was point man for the Arab world in four major modern wars with the state of Israel. The Arab coalition enjoyed the advantage of superior numbers, firepower, transport and supplies, yet in each war were soundly defeated. Of course Israel alone didn't defeat Egypt and the others, the God of Israel did!

Egypt is like a woman in fear. The shattering fourfold defeat by Israel is called in Arabic, "al Nakba," "the disaster." Egypt is terrified of another war with Israel. The most populous Arab country also fears an Islamist take over. This prophecy of Egypt's fear was fulfilled in part by the humiliation of the 1967 rout. The Egyptian air force was rendered inoperative, more than 900 tanks destroyed, more than a tenth of the Egyptian army was killed, and the head of the Egyptian army committed suicide. Even Gamel Nasser resigned temporarily.

The Muslim brotherhood, the philosophical and ideological incubator of the current Islamic resurgence, is an Egyptian creation but has been heavily suppressed by the Egyptian government, from Nasser through Mubarak.

This is a nation whose state-sanctioned media thrives on

bizarre conspiracy theories, blaming every problem, shortcoming, or any other evil on the Jews (backed by the CIA of course!). *"The wicked flee when no one pursues them, but the Righteous are bold as a lion."* (Proverbs 28:1)

Recently during the Egyptian observance of the religious month of Ramadan, a television series was shown on state TV that featured the ancient Jewish blood libel, portraying Jews as stealing Arab children to drain them of their blood to make Matza bread. These people are afraid.

Muslim Egypt is an unrelenting enemy of Christianity and of Israel. Within days after the "revolution" that toppled the Mubarak regime, video was released of the Egyptian army attacking an unarmed Coptic monastery, shooting people, and pushing over the walls and gates of the monastery with armored personnel carriers. Frantic monks could be heard singing "Kyrie Eleison" (Greek for "Lord have mercy") in the background.

This is a nation that gave the world the Muslim Brotherhood, the grandfather of the modern, murderous Jihad. Al Azhar University is in Cairo, the Harvard and Cambridge of radical Sunni Islam. Al Azhar gives ideological support for Jihadist terror, being the intellectual engine of the current Muslim hate campaign against the west.

The lead hijacker of the 9-11 plot was an Egyptian, Mohammed Atta. An Egyptian pediatrician, Ayman Al Zawahiri, is the late Osama Bin Ladin's right-hand man. The Muslim world has, in the modern world, been radicalized by the writings of Egyptians Sayyid Qutb and Hassan Al Banna. In short, the Egyptian people are very influential in the current terrorization of the world in the name of Allah.

The real Egypt is not seen in the young Western-educated twenty-somethings waving cell phones and using Facebook to organize peace rallies. This is the wishful fantasy of Western liberalism. Rather, Egypt's face was seen in the rabid mob that

26

savagely assaulted Western journalists and used the riotous occasion to ravish women on the street in shocking depravity. As the two hundred men outraged a young Western woman on the public street, they chanted hatefully, "Jew, Jew, Jew!".

This from *Slate Magazine*, "A 2008 study found 83 percent of Egyptian women said they had been sexually harassed, while 62 percent of men admitted to harassing women; 53 percent of men blamed women for 'bringing it on themselves'. A shocking 97 percent of female foreign visitors to Egypt reported some level of sexual harassment." [By Sarah A. Topol, Posted Friday, Feb. 18, 2011, "Why Egyptian Women Are Demoralized By Lara Logan's Assault"]

Egypt has long countenanced the kidnapping of young Christian Coptic girls, to be "married" and registered as Muslims. This is a major form of 'Muslim evangelism' in this Sunni Muslim majority country! The Christian families have been turned away by police, and in some instances, prosecuted for complaining of such practices. Do they think the real God doesn't see this? Isaiah warns:

The burden of Egypt. Behold, the Lord rideth upon a swift cloud, and shall come into Egypt: and the idols of Egypt shall be moved at his presence, and the heart of Egypt shall melt in the midst of it. (Isaiah 19:1)

The Lord comes again to judge Egypt, in the last days, to make war once again on her idols as he did in the Exodus.

And I will set the Egyptians against the Egyptians: and they shall fight every one against his brother, and every one against his neighbour; city against city, and kingdom against kingdom. (Isaiah 19:2)

This verse was quoted by Jesus in Matthew 24 when he warned of the cataclysmic days of the tribulation. Egypt will suffer a civil war, as the whole world slips into chaos.

And the Egyptians will I give over into the hand of a cruel lord; and a fierce king shall rule over them, saith the Lord, the Lord of hosts. (Isaiah 19:4)

27

Could this be happening before our eyes? Mohammed Morsi's Egypt has already seen 'Koranic' executions such as beheadings and crucifixions occur within the first year of his reign.

The princes of Zoan are become fools, the princes of Noph are deceived; they have also seduced Egypt, even they that are the stay of the tribes thereof. The Lord hath mingled a perverse spirit in the midst thereof: and they have caused Egypt to err in every work thereof, as a drunken man staggereth in his vomit. (Isaiah 19:13-14)

As part of God's judgment on Egypt, He will confuse the reasoning of the leadership, setting the nation on a self-destructive path, as a judgment. Egypt has a time of reckoning coming before she can be healed. But, Egypt will eventually be healed:

Therefore thus saith the Lord GOD; Behold, I will bring a sword upon thee, and cut off man and beast out of thee. And the land of Egypt shall be desolate and waste; and they shall know that I am the LORD: because he hath said, The river is mine, and I have made it. Behold, therefore I am against thee, and against thy rivers, and I will make the land of Egypt utterly waste and desolate, from the tower of Syene even unto the border of Ethiopia. (Ezekiel 29:8-10)

Radical, violent, anti-West, anti-Christian, anti-Jewish Islam is going to rule over the largest Arab population in the world. Already, the newly liberated from Mubarek Egyptian population met in the streets of Cairo by the hundreds of thousands to hail the once exiled fundamentalist preacher, Qadrawi, who called for a march on Jerusalem.

Within days of toppling Mubarek, the Egyptian army was firing on unarmed Coptic monks and bulldozing their monastery. Mohammed al Baradai, former U.N. nuclear compliance official whom secularists hoped would head up a new Egyptian democracy, recently announced that Egypt didn't ever have a treaty with Israel, Mubarak did.

Something soon is going to happen in Egypt that is so awful, Egyptians will have to flee their own land and live as refugees. The land will be rendered uninhabitable for forty years!

No foot of man shall pass through it, nor foot of beast shall pass through it, neither shall it be inhabited forty years. And I will make the land of Egypt desolate in the midst of the countries that are desolate, and her cities among the cities that are laid waste shall be desolate forty years: and I will scatter the Egyptians among the nations, and will disperse them through the countries. (Ezekiel 29:11-12)

But prophecy asserts that Egypt will, in the end, turn to the living God and drop Islam once and for all. God says He will make Himself known to the Egyptians, and that they will turn to Him in a time of great distress. In mercy God will reveal himself to them.

And it shall be for a sign and for a witness unto the LORD of hosts in the land of Egypt: for they shall cry unto the LORD because of the oppressors, and he shall send them a saviour, and a great one, and he shall deliver them. And the LORD shall be known to Egypt, and the Egyptians shall know the LORD in that day, and shall do sacrifice and oblation; yea, they shall vow a vow unto the LORD, and perform it. (Isaiah 19:21-22)

Consequently the Egyptians will make peace with Israel, and after some time (probably during the Millennium), return *en masse* to their own land. They will be trading partners and brothers, the Egyptians, Israelis, and Iraqis.

In that day shall there be a highway out of Egypt to Assyria, and the Assyrian shall come into Egypt, and the Egyptian into Assyria, and the Egyptians shall serve with the Assyrians. In that day shall Israel be the third with Egypt and with Assyria, even a blessing in the midst of the land: Whom the LORD of hosts shall bless, saying, Blessed be Egypt my people, and Assyria the work of my hands, and Israel mine inheritance. (Isaiah 19:23-25)

Yet thus saith the Lord GOD; At the end of forty years will I gather the Egyptians from the people whither they were scattered. (Ezekiel 29:13)

In the Millennium, Egypt is directly addressed by the Lord Himself. He warns her to make sure she is in attendance at the Feast of Tabernacles, lest He withhold rain from her.

Then the survivors from all the nations that have attacked Jerusalem will go up year after year to worship the King, the LORD Almighty, and to celebrate the Festival of Tabernacles. If any of the peoples of the earth do not go up to Jerusalem to worship the King, the LORD Almighty, they will have no rain. If the Egyptian people do not go up and take part, they will have no rain." (Zec 14:17, 18)

Chapter 6 – Damascus and Syria

The burden of Damascus:

Behold, Damascus is taken away from being a city, and it shall be a ruinous heap. The cities of Aroer are forsaken: they shall be for flocks, which shall lie down, and none shall make them afraid.

(Isaiah 17:2)

Damascus is known as the oldest continuously occupied city in the world. The prophets Elijah and Elisha went there to minister to Assyrian kings. The blinded Saul of Tarsus was led by the hand to a home on Damascus's Straight Street, where he found his Messiah and recovered his sight. That very street still exists in Damascus.

This ancient city has a rich history spanning thousands of years, encompassing influxes of Assyrians, Babylonians, Romans, Crusaders, Byzantines and Muslims. The population of Damascus currently is about 85 percent Muslim, 10 percent Christian, and five percent other. But according to scripture, the city is doomed to utter destruction in the last days, as are several other Arab cities.

Presently, Damascus is the capital of Syria, which is ruled by Bashir Assad, a secular Arab leader, but also an implacable enemy of Israel. Assad's Ba'athist ruling party is a relic of the pan-Arabist, fascist, secular experiments of the 1960s and '70s. The other notable Ba'athist government was Saddam Hussein's Iraq, which has since been dismantled. Assad is an Alawite Muslim, but his rule has been secular. Assad's Syria has been a harshly ruled police state, with the Alawite minority ruling over the Sunni majority, breeding much resentment.

Bashir Assad's father, Hafez, waged a decades-long war against the Muslim Brotherhood, at one time even cordoning off large sections of Hama (Syria's fourth largest city, and a long time Muslim Brotherhood stronghold) and carpet bombing entire sectors where Brotherhood sympathizers lived, killing 20,000. Bulldozers leveled the rubble of what were once teeming neighborhoods. Bashir

Assad is following in his father's bloody footprints, having killed 30,000 of his own people in a brutal suppression of the Syrian version of the "Arab Spring." The Assads are Alawite Muslims, a minority offshoot of Shia Islam, clinging to power over a vast Sunni majority. Assad's Syria is an ally of Iran, Israel's bitter enemy. It is also an ally and client of Russia.

Perhaps part of the judgment coming upon Damascus has to do with its implacable enmity with Israel. Every major Islamic terrorist group is allowed to headquarter openly in Damascus. Syria has participated in four major wars against Israel and continuously wages proxy wars against her through Hamas, Hezbullah, and Palestinian Islamic Jihad. There is constant tension between Israel and Syria over the Golan Heights, seized by Israel in the 1967 Six Day War. The Syrians had been using the heights to shell Jewish villages in Galilee.

In September 2007, the world was surprised at the news that Israeli war planes took out the al-Kibar nuclear facility in Syria. Israeli Intelligence had noted that Syria had been visited by Abdul Khan, the father of Pakistan's nuclear program, and had closely monitored the near completion of the nuclear facility, according to an article in the Jewish Policy Center, *The Attack on Syria's Al khibar Facility.*

In hindsight, there were several warnings in recent years that Syria might be pursuing nuclear weapons. The December 2001 National

Intelligence Estimate, focusing on foreign missile development, noted the U.S. intelligence community's concerns about "Syria's intentions regarding nuclear weapons." An unclassified 2004 report by the Deputy Director of National Intelligence for Analysis stated that Pakistani investigators had confirmed that Abdul Qadeer Khan—the Pakistani nuclear scientist who ran a clandestine black market network—offered "nuclear technology and hardware to Syria."

The report expressed concern "that expertise or technology could have been transferred." Press reports also began to circulate in 2004 that Khan had visited Syria on several occasions, and had met with senior Syrian officials in Iran. While Syria denied this, Bashar al-Assad acknowledged in a 2007 interview with an Austrian newspaper that he had received a letter from Khan in 2001. He claimed that he rebuffed the overture, unsure "if it was an Israeli trap."

The Syrian reaction to the Israeli attack was unusually timid, according to the same article. Syria's response in the wake of Israel's bombing was curious. The regime sought no retaliatory measures. It did not even ask the U.N. Security Council to discuss or condemn the incident. Rather, satellite photos show Syria's efforts to scrub the site of any traces of the nuclear reactor that Syria denied having. Reuters reported that Syria bulldozed the area, "removed debris and erected a new building in a possible cover-up." Former U.N. weapons inspector, David Albright, president of the prestigious Institute for Science and International Security (ISIS), told the New York Times:

> It looks like Syria is trying to hide something and destroy the evidence of some activity. But it won't work. Syria has got to answer questions about what it was doing.

> As of late the winds of the "Arab Spring" are blowing in Syria. However the longing for freedom from Assad's police state is being countered by the sheer brutality of the Syrian regime. Thousands of people have died as a result of the Government suppression of street protests. [Daveed Gartenstein-Ross and Joshua D Goodman, Infocus Quarterly, Jewish Policy Center]

Nightmarish reports are coming out of Syria of military assaults on civilians, massacres of defecting soldiers, thousands of refugees fleeing to Turkey and Lebanon, political murders, atrocities, tortures of civilians and even children. At this point, the outcome is unknown as to whether Syria will fall into the hands of the Muslim Brotherhood or remain a Ba-athist police state. But we do know that Syria plays a major role in the end-times scenario, as Isaiah prophesied:

The burden of Damascus. Behold, Damascus is taken away from being a city, and it shall be a ruinous heap. The cities of Aroer are forsaken: they shall be for flocks, which shall lie down, and none shall make them afraid. (Isaiah 17:1-2)

A dreadful thing that has not ever happened in history is about to occur: Damascus will cease from being a city; no longer will it be a seat of government, as a heap of rubble is its future.

Jeremiah implies that shortly before her destruction, Damascus will be surprised that Jerusalem is not "deserted" as she expected. This causes Damascus to lose heart herself.

Damascus has grown feeble; he turns to flee, and fear has seized her. Anguish and sorrows have taken her like a woman in labor. Why is the city of praise not deserted, the city of My joy? Therefore her young men shall fall in her streets, and all the men of war shall be cut off in that day, says the LORD of hosts. I will kindle a fire in the wall of Damascus, And it shall consume the palaces of Ben-Hadad. (Jeremiah 49:24-27)

Whatever the provocation, the destruction of Damascus will reflect badly upon Israel in the court of world opinion. The world will turn on Israel, blaming her for what happens to Damascus. What little favor Israel had enjoyed up until then will shrivel up; it will resemble the last few olives left after the shaking of the olive tree by the reapers.

In that day it shall come to pass that the glory of Jacob will wane, and the fatness of his flesh grow lean. It shall be as when the harvester gathers the grain, and reaps the heads with his arm; it shall be as he who gathers heads of grain in the Valley of Rephaim. Yet gleaning grapes will be left in it, like the shaking of an olive tree, two or three olives at the top of the uppermost bough, four or five in its most fruitful branches, says the LORD God of Israel. (Isaiah 17:4-6)

Damascus shall be obliterated in the context of a wider war, which will be destructive of other Arab cities as well, such as the area we call Gaza, which is a terrorist state designated as part of the U.N.-imposed "two state solution," but which God calls, "the nation not desired."

Gather yourselves together, yes, gather together, undesirable nation, before the decree is issued, the day passes like chaff, before the LORD's fierce anger comes upon you, before the day of the LORD's anger comes upon you! (Zechariah 2:1-2)

For Gaza shall be forsaken, and Ashkelon desolate; they shall drive out Ashdod at noonday, and Ekron shall be uprooted. Woe to the inhabitants of the seacoast, the nation of the Cherethites! The word of the LORD is against you, Canaan, land of the Philistines. (Zephaniah 2:4-5)

The one positive aspect of these terrible times is that even the hardest of men will begin to seek the living God:

In that day a man will look to his Maker, and his eyes will have respect for the Holy One of Israel. (Isaiah 17:7)

Zechariah echoes Isaiah:

The burden of the word of the LORD in the land of Hadrach, and Damascus shall be the rest thereof: when the eyes of man, as of all the tribes of Israel, shall be toward the LORD. (Zechariah 9:1)

The international outcry that will be raised against Israel will be unprecedented. The nations line up to register complaint in the U.N., newspaper headlines will scream, pundits will wax eloquent with moral indignation, religious leaders will pontificate against Israel, her former lovers will leave her, and it will be extremely unfashionable to stand with God's chosen people in that day.

Woe to the multitude of many people who make a noise like the roar of the seas, and to the rushing of nations that make a rushing like the rushing of mighty waters! The nations will rush like the rushing of many waters. (Isaiah 17:11-12)

But the outcry will merely be the prelude to the outpouring of divine wrath upon all nations. Tribulation such as never occurred upon the earth, the wind and the sea raging, and men's hearts failing them for fear...

But God will rebuke them and they will flee far away, and be chased like the chaff of the mountains before the wind, like a rolling thing before the whirlwind. (Isaiah 17: 13-14)

But it is as in the evening, which seems always darkest before dawn, such is the tribulation and time of Jacob's trouble, as Isaiah says:

Then behold, at eventide, trouble! And before the morning, he is no more. This is the portion of those who plunder us, and the lot of those who rob us. (Isaiah 17:14)

Chapter 7 – Jordan: Ammon, Moab and Edom

No longer will the people of Israel have malicious neighbors who are painful briers and sharp thorns. Then they will know that I am the Sovereign LORD.

(Ezekiel 28:24)

The Bible makes no reference to a national entity by the name of Jordan, because the modern nation called Jordan is a relatively recent creation. The British and French victors of the first World War divided the Middle East as the spoils of the Ottoman empire, which had sided with the Germans. By writing lines on maps, British and French diplomats created the 'nations' of Jordan, Iraq, Syria, Lebanon and others. The victors of World War I also set up and maintained their preferred Middle Eastern kings and kingdoms.

Arabia was once ruled by the royal Hashemite family, who claim direct descent from Mohammed and Fatimah. But the Hashemites were driven out of Arabia by the now ruling Saud family. The British allotted the rule over the newly created nation, "Jordan," to the Hashemites who rule over it to this day.

Biblically, that land is known as Ammon, Moab and Edom and is of great significance in Bible prophecy. The Ammonites and Moabites were the children born of incest by Lot and his daughters after they fled Sodom and Gomorrah. Edom is the land given by God to Esau and his seed. Traditionally, these three nations, though related to Israel, have been her enemies.

Ammon is a reference to the northern third of the modern state of Jordan, bordered on the west by the Jordan river. It is currently antagonistic to Israel, but in a "cold peace." King Abdullah, of the Hashemite family that rules Jordan, has the distinction in the Arab world of being known as the direct descendant of the 'prophet' Mohammed.

Concerning the Ammonites, thus saith the LORD; Hath Israel no sons? hath he no heir? why then doth their king inherit Gad, and his people dwell in his cities? (Jeremiah 49:1)

The God of Israel wonders out loud in irony, aren't there enough children being born to Israel that Ammonites inhabit the cities of Gad? Gad is the eastern bank of the Jordan River that was, in Biblical times, the territory of Reuben, Gad and the half tribe of Manasseh.

But the King James obscures an important aspect of this statement by God, for according to the New American Standard Bible, God asks, "Why does Malcam possess Gad?" In other words, how is it that "Jordanians" possess the God-given territory of the children of Israel, in the name of a false god, (Malcam = Moloch)?

Therefore, behold, the days come, saith the LORD, that I will cause an alarm of war to be heard in Rabbah of the Ammonites; and it shall be a desolate heap, and her daughters shall be burned with fire: then shall Israel be heir unto them that were his heirs, saith the LORD. (Jeremiah 49:2)

Ammon, Moab and Edom all feature in the doomed 'Psalm 83' war, referred to as "the children of Lot, and Edom." War sirens will be heard in Rabbah, which is known now as Amman, Jordan. The city is slated for destruction. Like Damascus, it shall be turned into a "desolate heap." There will no longer be a "West Bank" controversy, for, as a result of God's judgment on Ammon, Israel shall retake the territory of the east bank of the Jordan.

Howl, O Heshbon, for Ai is spoiled: cry, ye daughters of Rabbah, gird you with sackcloth; lament, and run to and fro by the hedges; for their king shall go into captivity, and his priests and his princes together. (Jeremiah 49:3)

Once again, the New American Standard Bible is helpful, for it tells us that "Malcam shall go into captivity, with his priests and princes." Malcam, or Moloch, is just another demonic god worshiped by the pagan Arabs and currently masquerades as Allah.

Because Ammon rejoiced over Israel's many calamities, and partook of the everlasting hatred of Israel, according to Ezekiel also, Ammon is to suffer destruction:

For this is what the Sovereign LORD says: Because you have clapped your hands and stamped your feet, rejoicing with all the malice of your heart against the land of Israel, therefore I will stretch out my hand against you and give you as plunder to the nations. I will wipe you out from among the nations and exterminate you from the countries. I will destroy you, and you will know that I am the LORD. (Ezekiel 25:6-7)

But the destruction will not be total for Ammon, for He promises them in Ezekiel, "You will know that I am the LORD," and in Jeremiah, the refugees of northern Jordan will be brought back to the land!

Behold, I will bring a fear upon thee, saith the Lord GOD of hosts, from all those that be about thee; and ye shall be driven out every man right forth; and none shall gather up him that wandereth. And afterward I will bring again the captivity of the children of Ammon, saith the LORD. (Jeremiah 49:5-6)

Moab, or central Jordan, is slated for destruction at the coming of Jesus. Isaiah 25 has Israel hiding and longing for Jesus. At the breaking of the day of His return, Israel celebrates the Savior and His salvation,

And it shall be said in that day, Lo, this is our God; we have waited for him, and he will save us: this is the LORD; we have waited for him, we will be glad and rejoice in his salvation. (Isaiah 25:9)

But the next verses have Jesus's foot on Moab's neck, as he is made to swim in a dunghill…

For in this mountain shall the hand of the LORD rest, and Moab shall be trodden down under him, even as straw is trodden down for the dunghill. And he shall spread forth his hands in the midst of them, as he that swimmeth spreadeth forth his hands to

swim: and he shall bring down their pride together with the spoils of their hands. And the fortress of the high fort of thy walls shall he bring down, lay low, and bring to the ground, even to the dust. (Isaiah 25:10-12)

Both Isaiah and Jeremiah mourn Moab and lament that her pride was her undoing. The destruction coming upon her is frightening.

Fear, and the pit, and the snare, shall be upon thee, O inhabitant of Moab, saith the LORD. He that fleeth from the fear shall fall into the pit; and he that getteth up out of the pit shall be taken in the snare: for I will bring upon it, even upon Moab, the year of their visitation, saith the LORD. (Jeremiah 47:43-44)

But the destruction of North and central Jordan will not be complete, for we are told that, like Ammon, a remnant of Moab will repent and be saved.

Yet will I bring again the captivity of Moab in the latter days, saith the LORD. Thus far is the judgment of Moab. (Jeremiah 47:48)

Southern Jordan, Edom or Mt. Sier, is slated for perhaps the grimmest judgment; it shall be rendered, in places, utterly uninhabitable. Obadiah and Ezekiel 35 both direct their focus on Edom, as representative of the perpetual hatred against Israel they have nourished.

Son of man, set thy face against mount Seir, and prophesy against it; And say unto it, Thus saith the Lord GOD; Behold, O mount Seir, I am

against thee, and I will stretch out mine hand against thee, and I will make thee most desolate. I will lay thy cities waste, and thou shalt be desolate, and thou shalt know that I am the LORD. Because thou hast had a perpetual hatred, and hast shed the blood of the children of Israel by the force of the sword in the time of their calamity, in the time that their iniquity had an end: Therefore, as I live, saith the Lord GOD, I will prepare thee unto blood, and blood shall pursue thee: sith thou hast not hated blood, even blood shall pursue thee. Thus will I make mount Seir most desolate, and cut off from it him that passeth out and him that returneth. (Ezekiel 35:2-7)

Obadiah tells us that God remembered the help Edom gave to oppressors of Israel over the years, barring their escapes, rejoicing in their calamities, possessing their vacated lands, and in particular the temple mount!

For thy violence against thy brother Jacob shame shall cover thee, and thou shalt be cut off for ever. In the day that thou stoodest on the other side, in the day that the strangers carried away captive his forces, and foreigners entered into his gates, and cast lots upon Jerusalem, even thou wast as one of them. But thou shouldest not have looked on the day of thy brother in the day that he became a stranger; neither shouldest thou have rejoiced over the children of Judah in the day of their destruction; neither shouldest thou have spoken proudly in the day of distress. (Obadiah 1:10-12)

Pray for the Muslim people, that they will indeed come to know the Lord, for these prophecies are given that all people might see what is happening and repent of their sins and call upon the name of the true and living God while there is still time. God is not willing for any to perish, but for all to come to repentance. "Whosoever will call upon the name of the Lord (Jesus who died for their sins) will be saved...."

Chapter 8 – Tyre and Sidon Equals Southern Lebanon

Yea, and what have ye to do with me, O Tyre, and Zidon, and all the coasts of Palestine? will ye render me a recompence?
and if ye recompense me, swiftly and speedily will I return your recompence upon your own head; (Joel 3:4)

As we stated earlier, an interesting exercise for Bible readers is to take the geographical predictions of the Hebrew prophets and transpose the ancient place names with modern place names; for example, Ammon would be Jordan, so would Moab and Edom, Elam would be Iran, Persia also is Iran, Assyria would be part of Iran and part of Iraq, Babylon proper is Iraq.

In this end-times scenario, God directly addresses "Tyre and Sidon" in a menacing fashion, challenging them to take vengeance upon Him if they can. Tyre and Sidon and the "coasts of Philistia," as the passage relates, is the area we know of as southern Lebanon and Gaza.

Lebanon has long been known as the only Christian country in the Middle East. Christianity in Lebanon goes back to Jesus Himself, who healed the daughter of a Syro-Phoenician woman in Matthew's Gospel, chapter 15.

For centuries, Christian sects such as the Maronites, Melkites, Greek Orthodox and Roman Catholics, Syrian Orthodox and Protestants constituted the majority in the land of the ancient Phoenicians. But in our own lifetime, things have changed dramatically. Decades before 9-11 woke America to the reality of the international war against humanity that Islam is waging, Lebanon suffered a campaign of "ethnic cleansing" of Christians by Muslims.

Christian villages were assaulted and centuries-old Christian communities had been broken up and/or destroyed by well-armed and supported Muslim militias, driving many Christians out of the country. Mercenaries from across the Muslim world streamed into Lebanon in the 1970s in order to take part in a jihad of pillage and murder.

From southern Lebanon, through the 1970s and early 1980s, the terrorist group the PLO would often launch border raids upon Israel, terrorizing and killing many innocent Israelis and others. The provocations increased until they became intolerable, and the U.N. proved impotent to stem the slaughter along Israel's northern border. In June 1982, Israel launched "Operation Peace For Galilee," an invasion of Lebanon that stopped just short of Beirut. There, the U.N. stepped in and saved Yasser Arafat and the remnant of his shattered army, shipping them off to Tunisia, allowing them to regroup, to live and terrorize for many other days. Israel occupied southern Lebanon, making the area a sanctuary for Christian refugees from the jihad in Lebanon.

But in May of 2000, Israel voted to withdraw from Lebanon, wearying of the steady casualty count, primarily due to the terrorist activity of the Iranian/Syrian-backed group Hezbollah. As Israel withdrew, Hezbollah became brazen in advancing, thus giving the Arab world the delusion that they had driven Israel out of southern Lebanon. Thus Hezbollah, and in particular its spokesman Sayyad Nasrallah, have become "rock stars" throughout the Muslim world for being the first to impose defeat on the modern state of Israel.

Nasrallah has become outspoken in his pledge to wipe out the state of Israel and feels emboldened by his recent "successes." Hezbollah has actually become a legitimate part of the government of Lebanon and has been stockpiling 40,000 rockets to rain upon Israel. Here are some of his statements:

"Palestine, from the sea to the river, is the property of Arabs and Palestinians and no one has the right to give up even a single grain of earth or one stone, because every grain of the land is holy. The entire land must be returned to its rightful owners."

43

"Could Israel be wiped out of existence? Yes, and a thousand times yes."

"If they [the Jews] all gather in Israel, it will save us the trouble of going after them worldwide."

"[Israel is] a cancer that needs to be removed at its roots."

"Our weapons, our blood and our rockets are all yours [the Palestinians] too, and we will we stay with you until we can pray with you at the Al-Aqsa mosque in united Jerusalem, capital of all of Palestine!"

Could the Holy God be addressing Hezbollah when He singles out "Tyre and Sidon" (i.e., southern Lebanon) in Joel 3? *"Will you avenge yourself upon me Tyre and Sidon? See how I will avenge myself on you!"*

Nasrallah and the terrorist group Hezbollah, which have insinuated themselves into the vacuum of southern Lebanon by the withdrawal of Israel, have been boasting of their upcoming total victory over Israel and Israel's God. We will see soon enough how that turns out.

Lebanon itself has a wonderful future, for it will be incorporated into the renewed state of Israel. I quote Arnold Fruchtenbaum's article, *The Arab States In Prophecy*, by which I have received much inspiration for this work:

"Peace between Israel and Lebanon will come by means of occupation." In Ezekiel 47:13 - 48:29 we are given the boundaries of the nation of Israel in the Messianic Kingdom. The tracing of the northern boundary shows that Israel will encompass all of modern-day Lebanon.

Chapter 9 – The New Amalekites

And the LORD said unto Moses, Write this for a memorial in a book, and rehearse it in the ears of Joshua: for I will utterly put out the remembrance of Amalek from under heaven. And Moses built an altar, and called the name of it Jehovah nissi: For he said, Because the LORD hath sworn that the LORD will have war with Amalek from generation to generation.
(Exodus 17:14-16)

Do you remember the Amalekites? These descendants of Esau were the terrorists of the book of Exodus. Rather than waging a frontal assault on the children of Israel, Amalekites staged raids on the weak, sick, lagging members of the congregation and slaughtered them without mercy.

God definitely wanted Israel to remember them: *Remember what Amalek did unto thee by the way, when ye were come forth out of Egypt; How he met thee by the way, and smote the hindmost of thee, even all that were feeble behind thee, when thou wast faint and weary; and he feared not God.*
(Deuteronomy 25:17-18)

We were reminded of the Amalekites again recently when the news came out about the terrorist assault on a Jewish family in Judea. The Udi Fogel family was murdered in cold blood by members of the militant wing of the Al Aqsa martyrs' brigade, of the Fatah political party. While the Fogels slept or read in their own beds, terrorists slipped into a home, stabbed a three-year-old in the heart, slit the throats of an infant, an eleven-year-old reading in bed, and his sleeping father. They then slaughtered the children's mother as she came out of her own bathroom.

Citizens of the doomed "Palestinian" state of Gaza held street celebrations over the murders, passing out candies and dancing for joy in the streets. These are the modern Amalekites. They may or may not be physical descendants of Esau's grandson, Amalek, but they operate in the character of an Amalekite. Celebrating the stabbing of a three-year-old by grown men? Passing out candies for joy over the slitting on an infant's throat?

We have been discussing the fate of Arab nations in Bible prophecy, for the Lord has much to say about the inhabitants of what was once known as Ammon, Moab, Edom, Tyre, Damascus, Persia, Lebanon, Egypt and Libya.

There is an expression in scripture, a Hebraism, which calls certain ones "Sons of..." this or that. The two disciples of Jesus were nicknamed "sons of thunder" for their temper. The Antichrist is called "The son of perdition" because he is already damned. In other words, this is not a reference to biological descent, rather it means one who is "in the character of" a person or trait. The Arab Muslim world operates in the character of Ishmael, who hated Isaac, and in the character of Esau, who felt cheated by and vowed to murder Jacob. Islam has taken up this "perpetual hatred".

Islamic terror causes these people who perpetrate such atrocities and those who openly celebrate them, to be "sons of Amalek." God told Moses and Joshua that He Himself would be at war perpetually with Amalek.

Because the LORD hath sworn that the LORD will have war with Amalek from generation to generation. (Exodus 17:18)

These nations, who jeered and celebrated in Israel's calamities time after time in the wanton slaughter, dispossession, and terror of the Jews in the land God promised them, are noted by the God of Israel and marked for judgment.

This is a direct word to these gloaters in the book of Obadiah:

For thy violence against thy brother Jacob shame shall cover thee, and thou shalt be cut off for ever... But thou shouldest not have looked on the day of thy brother in the day that he became a stranger; neither shouldest thou have rejoiced over the children of Judah in the day of their destruction; neither shouldest thou have spoken proudly in the day of distress. (Obadiah 10-12)

We need to pray that God will have mercy on these people and grant them the ability to see that they are in a satanic religion and on their way to hell. Islam is a murderous deception that obviously snuffs out the humanity of its worshipers in proportion to the devotion of its adherents.

But we have all heard the countless redeeming stories of Palestinians, such as the Hassan Yusef Massab (*Son of Hamas*) and Walid Shoebat, who have found the saving grace of God in Jesus Christ and obtained the forgiveness of sins and eternal life.

Chapter 10 – Who is Edom?
Why is He Doomed?

Who is this that cometh from Edom, with dyed garments from Bozrah? this that is glorious in his apparel, travelling in the greatness of his strength? I that speak in righteousness, mighty to save. Wherefore art thou red in thine apparel, and thy garments like him that treadeth in the winefat? I have trodden the wine-press alone; and of the people there was none with me: for I will tread them in mine anger, and trample them in my fury; and their blood shall be sprinkled upon my garments, and I will stain all my raiment. For the day of vengeance is in mine heart, and the year of my redeemed is come. (Isaiah 63:1-4)

How important is the Arab world to Bible prophecy? Isaiah predicts that Jesus Himself comes to His own people from Edom, which is the territory south and east of the Dead Sea, currently known as southern Jordan and northern Saudi Arabia. In the process of saving his people, Jesus' garments become spattered in the blood of God's enemies, who sought to annihilate those people.

Such is the day of divine vengeance, and the time of the redemption of the "seed of the woman." It starts in Edom and works its way out to the whole world, ending in the judgment of the nations and the establishment of the Kingdom of God.

Israel, besieged and surrounded, will be rescued on that day by her redeemer/husband, the LORD.

Behold, the day of the Lord cometh, and thy spoil shall be divided in the midst of thee. For I will gather all nations against Jerusalem to battle; and the city shall be taken, and the houses rifled, and the women ravished; and half of the city shall go forth into captivity, and the residue of the people shall not be cut off from the city. Then shall the Lord go forth, and fight against those nations, as when he fought in the day of battle. And his feet shall stand in that day upon the mount of Olives... (Zechariah 14:1-4)

Edom, or Esau as he is known, was Jacob's twin brother. He was the firstborn, the son expected by man to have the birthright. But the birthright of Abraham and Isaac, which involved the very purpose of God for the salvation of the world, was a matter of God's choosing, not man's.

God didn't choose Esau to bring into the world the Messiah, the promised "seed of the woman." God chose the secondborn, Jacob. The Messiah would be the God of Abraham, Isaac and Jacob. Esau could have accepted this; he could also have entered into the salvation of God, by faith, as Abraham did. But instead of humbly accepting God's choice, Esau cultivated a sense of grievance, which turned into bitterness. He hated Jacob and vowed to murder him, believing that Jacob had swindled him out of his birthright. The descendants of Esau have also nurtured that hatred; in fact, it exists to this day, and it is called in scripture, "the Perpetual hatred."

Edom has long been destroyed as a national entity, as has Moab and Ammon. They are no longer kingdoms as they once were. But there are a people whom God addresses as Edom (or Esau, or Mt. Sier) who feature heavily in end times prophecy. The descendant Ishmaelites, Edomites, Moabites, Midianites, and the rest of the traditional, ancient enemies of Israel constitute the Arab Middle East. A good many have been Christianized, but the bulk of them are Muslim. I believe that Edom is a designation for the Arab Muslim world who are the near neighbors of Israel and who hate her very existence.

The prophet Obadiah addresses the coming judgment on Esau, and gives the reasons why:

Violence against his brother Jacob – *For thy violence against thy brother Jacob shame shall cover thee, and thou shalt be cut off for ever.*
(Obadiah 1:10)

Joining those who plundered Jerusalem - *In the day that thou stoodest on the other side, in the day that the strangers carried* *away captive his forces, and foreigners entered into his gates, and cast lots upon Jerusalem, even thou wast as one of them.* (Obadiah 1:11)

Taking Joy in the suffering and humiliation of Israel – *But thou shouldest not have looked on the day of thy brother in the day that he became a stranger; neither shouldest thou have rejoiced over the children of Judah in the day of their destruction; neither shouldest thou have spoken proudly in the day of distress.* (Obadiah 1:13)

We see shades of this in the recent spectacle of "Palestinian" Arabs dancing in the streets and passing out sweets at the news of the slaughter of the Udi Fogel family in their beds, including the slitting of an infant's throat, and the stabbing of a three-year-old in the heart by grown men. God has seen this and taken note.

Assisting the persecutors of Israel and hindering their escape from them – The Hadiths of the Koran teach Muslims that this very thing will be done in the last days, that even the rocks and trees will betray the hiding places of Jews, that they might be slaughtered.

No wonder then that Esau's modern sons were so willing to assist the Nazis in the holocaust, by rioting and pogroms, to prevent their return to the Holy Land in the days of the Nazi terror. This is the murderous rage of Edom, called the "perpetual hatred" in Ezekiel.

Loving bloodshed – *Because thou hast had a perpetual hatred, and hast shed the blood of the children of Israel by the force of the sword in the time of their calamity, in the time that their iniquity had an end: Therefore, as I live, saith the Lord GOD, I will prepare thee unto blood, and blood shall pursue thee: sith [since] thou hast not hated blood, even blood shall pursue thee.* (Ezekiel 35:5-6)

Esau's spiritual descendants boast that they love blood. They name city squares in Gaza and the West Bank after mass murderers, and pass out sweets when Jewish children are murdered. Mothers aspire that their sons will be mass murderers and hold wedding ceremonies for them after they perform cruel murder.

They tell us in the West that they will prevail, because we love life but they love death. Should we even imagine that God doesn't see this and hate it? Christ will have the last word, not the USA or the EU.

Edom is sick, it is doomed; Christ is coming to make war on it. This death and blood-loving culture will be pursued by blood in the day that Christ comes back.

Claiming the Holy Mountain as theirs – *And thou shalt know that I am the LORD, and that I have heard all thy blasphemies which thou hast spoken against the mountains of Israel, saying, They are laid desolate, they are given us to consume. Thus with your mouth ye have boasted against me, and have multiplied your words against me: I have heard them.* (Ezekiel 35:12-13)

In the aftermath of the 1967 Six-Day War and the retaking of Jerusalem, the victorious Israelis granted stewardship of the newly acquired temple mount, Israel's holiest site, to the Jordanian Waqf. The sanctity of this mountain to those who believe in the Bible is incalculable. The temple mount is the only place on earth where God says He has placed His name, yet it is currently controlled by Edomites. Jesus did say that "Jerusalem would be trodden underfoot of the gentiles until the time of the gentiles be fulfilled."

They are feverishly destroying any archeological evidence of a Jewish temple, hollowing out the Holy Mountain, and hauling off the rubble containing crushed but precious relics of first and second temple, and dumping them as landfill! God is allowing this until the appointed time.

From an *Arutz Sheva* article:

"A group of Jews that ascended the Temple Mount Sunday were shocked to see that ancient beams of wood that had apparently been used during the period of the Holy Temple were being used as firewood by Arabs on the Mount, and off it. Archaeologists have dated the wood as far back as the First Temple period, and appear to be among the celebrated "Cedars of Lebanon" mentioned in the

Tanach.

"The wood, consisting of giant beams, first appeared at the end of the 1930s, when the Al-Aqsa mosque which currently occupies the Temple Mount was refurbished. The beams had been used in the roof structure of the mosque, and already at that time they were said to be thousands of years old by archaeologists – preserved only because they had been used in the building. Some of the beams were dated to the first Temple period, others to Roman times, and at least one beam was found to have Byzantine-era designs etched on it." (Arabs Burning Cedars, David Lev *Arutz Sheva* 11/04/2012)

Therefore thus saith the Lord GOD; Surely in the fire of my jealousy have I spoken against the residue of the heathen, and against all Idumea, which have appointed my land into their possession with the joy of all their heart, with despiteful minds, to cast it out for a prey. (Ezekiel 36:5)

Judgment is coming to Edom. There are places in southern Jordan that are going to be rendered uninhabitable even into the Millennium, so great is the divine wrath soon to be revealed upon Edom. Christ himself will return via Edom, because in the end, his own people, Israel, are trapped there surrounded by the nations, hunted and slain wherever found, and living in booths. He comes to rescue them.

Pray for the Muslims, the Arab people; many are being converted by dreams, visions and revelations of Jesus. God is not willing that any should perish but that all should come to repentance. Whosoever will call upon the name of Jesus will be saved!

Chapter 11 – Habbakuk's Vision; God Came From Teman

God came from Teman, and the Holy One from mount Paran. [Selah]. His glory covered the heavens, and the earth was full of his praise. And his brightness was as the light; he had horns coming out of his hand: and there was the hiding of his power. Before him went the pestilence, and burning coals went forth at his feet. He stood, and measured the earth: he beheld, and drove asunder the nations; and the everlasting mountains were scattered, the perpetual hills did bow: his ways are everlasting. I saw the tents of Cushan in affliction: and the curtains of the land of Midian did tremble. (Habbakuk 3:4-7)

Habbakuk was troubled by the immorality of his own people, Judah. When he petitioned the LORD, God assured him that He too was concerned about Judah and was going to use the Babylonians to punish them. This provoked a second complaint by Habbakuk, "How could God use a people worse than Judah, the idolatrous Babylonians, to punish back-slidden Judah?"

God's answer was a revelation, that there were only two kinds of people on the earth: those who are proud and who live by pride and independence from God, and those who live their lives by faith in God and are justified. The just will live by faith in God. No matter what comes, those who truly fear God and rely on Him will live. But the proud, "the one whose heart is lifted up in himself," will be denied by God everything they crave and imagine that they can obtain by their own prowess.

Then Habbakuk is given a revelation of the ultimate settling of things, at the coming of the Lord in Glory, at the end of days. We are told that "God came from Teman," or literally, "God is coming from Teman." Where is Teman and why would God be coming from Teman? Teman was a district in the area now known as southern Jordan, but in ancient times was called Edom. Edom was the area

53

given to Jacob's twin, Esau, as his inheritance.

Esau, Isaac's favored, eldest son, was Isaac's choice for the blessing of Abraham, but he was not God's choice; Jacob was. In spite of Isaac's desire, Jacob received the blessing God had elected him to, but Esau always resented him for it, feeling he had been cheated out of it.

Esau went on to found a great people, the Edomites, but for the most part, it was a people estranged from the God of the Bible. They embraced the paganism of the Canaanites, worshipped false gods, and became a fierce, perpetual enemy of Israel. David and Solomon subdued them, but with the break-up of the Kingdom of Israel, they shook off the yoke of tribute to Israel.

The Edomites have been willing and avid participants in something called "the perpetual hatred" of Israel and the Jews. This hatred has been nurtured since the days of Esau and by his intermarriage with Ishmael's family. It is the resentment of perceived disenfranchisement, the feeling of being cheated out of home, land, inheritance, etc., by the evil Jews.

When the temple was destroyed, both in 589 BC and in 70 AD, the Edomites gleefully cooperated in Israel's destruction and enslavement, blocking routes of escape and pointing out hiding places, jeering the Jews as they were transported to the slave markets of the world.

The hatred is current and real, as this passage in Ezekiel proclaims in this prophecy against Edom:

Because thou hast had a perpetual hatred, and hast shed the blood of the children of Israel by the force of the sword in the time of their calamity, in the time that their iniquity had an end: Therefore, as I live, saith the Lord GOD, I will prepare thee unto blood, and blood shall pursue thee: sith thou hast not hated blood, even blood shall pursue thee. Thus will I make mount Seir most desolate, and cut off from it him that passeth out and him that returneth. (Ezekiel 35:5-7)

Amos also mentions it as a determining factor in the judgment upon them.

Thus saith the LORD; For three transgressions of Edom, and for four, I will not turn away the punishment thereof; because he did pursue his brother with the sword, and did cast off all pity, and his anger did tear perpetually, and he kept his wrath for ever: But I will send a fire upon Teman, which shall devour the palaces of Bozrah. (Amos 1:11-12)

After being subdued by Seleucids, Egyptians, and eventually the Jewish Hasmoneans, many of the Edomites actually converted to Judaism. It was from an Edomite family that Rome appointed governors over Judea, the Herods. Though brutal and paranoid as a leader, Herod the Great was so scrupulous about keeping kosher that Caesar is reported to have quipped that it was "safer to be Herod's pig, than to be his son" after Herod killed one of his own sons in a paranoid rage.

The Edomites would eventually seek to throw off the yoke of the Romans themselves and were subsequently crushed, bringing an end to their kingdom in 135 AD. But the descendants of Esau still inhabit the Middle East, having intermingled with the Arabs, and as of the seventh century, having embraced Islam.

It is Islam which is the current nourisher of the "everlasting hatred" of Israel, a hatred unto blood lust, as Ezekiel tells us. As I write this, Edomites all around the Middle East are celebrating with candies, gunfire, and gifts of food and drink, the ambush and killing of eight Israelis on a public bus.

In 2010, the sickening spectacle of sweets, gifts and gunfire in the streets was performed again to honor the treacherous break in and murder of the Uri Fogel family in their own beds. Edom rejoiced at the news, which included the slitting of an infant's throat!

Arab Islam (Edom) is oblivious to the wrath that awaits them; they think this is their time to conquer! They misjudge the timidity of the West and the decadence we have allowed to rot our societies. But God still says, "I will bless those who bless you and curse those who curse you (Israel)!"

In Habbakuk's vision, as well as in Isaiah's, God comes back to Edom first, then proceeds on to deliver the beleaguered remnant in the ravished Jerusalem. Those who are in Judea have had to flee their homes; they have had to run for their lives into the wilderness of what is now called Jordan; they are forced to live in tents as in the days of the Exodus.

The Muslim world sees this as their opportunity to finally wipe the Jews out, so they converge on the besieged people in the wilderness, believing that now finally is the time of vengeance, the time when Edom's hatred will finally be expressed, as the Hadiths of Islam proclaim of the last day:

"The last day cannot come until the Jews are hunted down and slaughtered. If a Jew hides behind a rock or a tree, even the rocks and trees will cry out, 'There is a Jew hiding here, come! kill him, O Muslim!'"

That is why God comes to Teman, to execute vengeance on Edom, and to deliver his people.

Thus saith the Lord GOD; Because that Edom hath dealt against the house of Judah by taking vengeance, and hath greatly offended, and revenged himself upon them; Therefore thus saith the Lord GOD; I will also stretch out mine hand upon Edom, and will cut off man and beast from it; and I will make it desolate from Teman; and they of Dedan shall fall by the sword. (Ezekiel 25:12-13)

Perhaps the most frightening picture of the coming of the Lord is in Isaiah 63, where he too says that God comes to us from Edom:

Who is this that cometh from Edom, with dyed garments from Bozrah? this that is glorious in his apparel, traveling in the greatness of his strength? I that speak in righteousness, mighty to save. Wherefore art thou red in thine apparel, and thy garments like him that treadeth in the wine-fat? I have trodden the wine-press alone; and of the people there was none with me: for I will tread them in mine anger, and trample them in my fury; and their blood shall be sprinkled upon my garments, and I will stain all my raiment.

56

For the day of vengeance is in mine heart, and the year of my redeemed is come. (Isaiah 63:1-4)

Pray for the Arab Muslim people; they have no idea the wrath that is stored up for them. We must love them and seek to reach them with the message of love and of warning. Anyone can be saved; Jesus died for all of us! May God have mercy on them and turn them unto Him!

Chapter 12–Southern and Northern Iraq: Assyria and Babylon.

The modern nation called Iraq is said to lie in the very cradle of civilization. Mesopotamia, "the land between two rivers," the Tigris and Euphrates, features prominently in the prophetic record. Biblically, it is referred to as Assyria, Shinar, and Babylon. The Biblical region of Assyria, which is northern Iraq and eastern Syria, has a bright future according to the prophets of the Bible. In the future Egypt, northern Iraq and Israel will be bound together by a common faith (Christianity) and by a highway for trade! God is good!

In that day shall there be a highway out of Egypt to Assyria, and the Assyrian shall come into Egypt, and the Egyptian into Assyria, and the Egyptians shall serve with the Assyrians. In that day shall Israel be the third with Egypt and with Assyria, even a blessing in the midst of the land: Whom the LORD of hosts shall bless, saying, Blessed be Egypt my people, and Assyria the work of my hands, and Israel mine inheritance. (Isaiah 19:23-25)

Just as the Egyptians are destined to do, the northern Iraqis will also shed the bondage of Islam all together and embrace the Gospel. Together with Israel and Egypt, they shall be saved and go into the Millennium as brothers, friends and partners.

Southern Iraq, i.e., Babylon, doesn't have such a rosy outlook. Parts of southern Iraq will be rendered uninhabitable by all but evil spirits even into the Millennium. Babylon is mentioned as often as Jerusalem is in the scriptures. The significance of Babylon lies on several levels.

Historically, Babylon is significant because it is the sight of the original worldwide rebellion against God at the Tower of Babel. There the peoples of the ancient world conspired against God in an unholy unity movement, in order to "make for themselves a name" and to create their own godless world order. Babylon is the place where human culture became diverse due to God's judgment in the confusion of languages. This is why Babylon is considered the oldest civilization, because it was from there that all other human civilizations emerged. All false religion can also be traced back to Babylon.

Babylon has yet to be punished for the destruction she wrought on the Temple of Solomon, an event that is commemorated yearly on Tishba'Av, as a national calamity for Israel. God ordained that the Babylonians be the ones to execute His judgment on His people, but He remembers her sins as well, having promised in Jeremiah that he would yet take vengeance for the destruction of His temple.

The voice of them that flee and escape out of the land of Babylon, to declare in Zion the vengeance of the Lord our God, the vengeance of his temple. (Jeremiah 50:28)

Geographically, Babylon is significant because much of the Biblical narrative takes place there. God allowed Nebuchadnessar, the Babylonian King, to be raised up as "His anointed" to judge Israel, destroying the temple in which they vainly trusted, and bringing the cream of the nation into captivity. Daniel and Ezekiel were written from Babylon.

Furthermore, she is spiritually significant, for Babylon represents the "city of man" – man's proud attempt at replacing God as center, building a tower that would "reach up unto heaven." Typologically, there are two world cities, Babylon and Jerusalem. Babylon the great is ever set against Jerusalem, the Holy City. Proud humanism, independent of God, versus humble worship, reliance upon the Creator and the acknowledgment of the need for a savior.

There is also an economic Babylon slated for destruction, as represented in Revelation chapter 18. In the vision, John saw Babylon represented as a world merchant mart, in which everything a person could lust after can be bought and sold, up to and including the very souls of men and women!

Alas, alas that great city Babylon, that mighty city! for in one hour is thy judgment come. And the merchants of the earth shall weep and mourn over her; for no man buyeth their merchandise any more: The merchandise of gold, and silver, and precious stones, and of pearls, and fine linen, and purple, and silk, and scarlet, and all thine wood, and all manner vessels of ivory, and all manner vessels of most precious wood, and of brass, and iron, and marble,

And cinnamon, and odours, and ointments, and frankincense, and wine, and oil, and fine flour, and wheat, and beasts, and sheep, and horses, and chariots, and slaves, and souls of men. And the fruits that thy soul lusted after are departed from thee, and all things which were dainty and goodly are departed from thee, and thou shalt find them no more at all. (Revelation 18:11-14)

There is also a religious Babylon, a gaudy Harlot, an obscene parody of the Bride of Christ. She is drunk on the blood of the true saints and clothed in the finest of luxuries, but she too is slated for destruction, as "the mother of all harlots and abominations."

Zechariah chapter 5 also indicates that Babylon will again be a center of world evil in the last days.

....And, behold, there was lifted up a talent of lead: and this is a woman that sitteth in the midst of the ephah. And he said, This is wickedness. And he cast it into the midst of the ephah; and he cast the weight of lead upon the mouth thereof. Then lifted I up mine eyes, and looked, and, behold, there came out two women, and the wind was in their wings; for they had wings like the wings of a stork: and they lifted up the ephah between the earth and the heaven. Then said I to the angel that talked with me, Whither do these bear the ephah? And he said unto me, To build it an house in the land of Shinar: and it shall be established, and set there upon her own base. (Zechariah 5:6-11)

Of course, there is a political Babylon, a renewed Tower of Babel, in which humanistic men, "the Kings of the earth and their rulers," seek to overthrow the verdict of the Most High and to unite the world in spite of the Babel judgment. This Babylon also is doomed to a devastating judgment, as Psalm 2 and Revelation 19 warn us. But we are concerned here with the prophecies directed to geographical Babylon.

Many would say that these prophecies have already been fulfilled in history, and indeed many of them have come to pass, but certainly not all. For example, Isaiah 13 is a prophecy that predicts Babylon being attacked by an international coalition, to destroy the whole land of Babylon.

The burden of Babylon, which Isaiah the son of Amoz did see.

Lift ye up a banner upon the high mountain, exalt the voice unto them, shake the hand, that they may go into the gates of the nobles. I have commanded my sanctified ones, I have also called my mighty ones for mine anger, even them that rejoice in my highness. The noise of a multitude in the mountains, like as of a great people; a tumultuous noise of the kingdoms of nations gathered together: the LORD of hosts mustereth the host of the battle. They come from a far country, from the end of heaven, even the LORD, and the weapons of his indignation, to destroy the whole land. (Isaiah 13:1-5)

How much destruction do they wreak? The land is to be rendered uninhabitable.

And Babylon, the glory of kingdoms, the beauty of the Chaldees' excellency, shall be as when God overthrew Sodom and Gomorrah. It shall never be inhabited, neither shall it be dwelt in from generation to generation: neither shall the Arabian pitch tent there; neither shall the shepherds make their fold there. (vs 19-20)

Jeremiah 50 and 51 also echo the prediction that Babylon would be invaded by a multinational confederation and rendered uninhabitable by men.

Therefore the wild beasts of the desert with the wild beasts of the islands shall dwell there, and the owls shall dwell therein: and it shall be no more inhabited for ever; neither shall it be dwelt in from generation to generation. As God overthrew Sodom and Gomorrah and the neighbour cities thereof, saith the LORD; so shall no man

61

abide there, neither shall any son of man dwell therein. Behold, a people shall come from the north, and a great nation, and many kings shall be raised up from the coasts of the earth. (Jeremiah 50:39-41)

Ancient Babylon wasn't destroyed as Sodom and Gommorah; it just fell into decay, and the land around it is still inhabited. These scriptures are yet to be fulfilled. Babylon, which is southern Iraq, is headed for judgment, which is final and irreversible.

Jeremiah the Prophet, after his prophetic warning of end times judgment on Egypt, Gaza, Jordan, Arabia, Syria, Persia, Syria, Gaza, and the Philistines, and ending in Iraq, i.e., Babylon, instructed his scribe Seruiah:

...When thou comest to Babylon, and shalt see, and shalt read all these words; Then shalt thou say, O LORD, thou hast spoken against this place, to cut it off, that none shall remain in it, neither man nor beast, but that it shall be desolate for ever. And it shall be, when thou hast made an end of reading this book, that thou shalt bind a stone to it, and cast it into the midst of Euphrates: And thou shalt say, Thus shall Babylon sink, and shall not rise from the evil that I will bring upon her: and they shall be weary. Thus far are the words of Jeremiah. (Jeremiah 51:61-64)

Such is the fate of southern Iraq, bitter enemy of Israel, persecutor of Christians, one time destroyer of the Temple, worshipper of false gods such as Allah. This hasn't occurred yet ,but it is sure to, for the mouth of the Lord has spoken it.

Like the scroll tied to a stone and thrown in the Euphrates, so shall Babylon fall and rise no more.

And a mighty angel took up a stone like a great millstone, and cast it into the sea, saying, Thus with violence shall that great city Babylon be thrown down, and shall be found no more at all. And the voice of harpers, and musicians, and of pipers, and trumpeters, shall be heard no more at all in thee; and no craftsman, of whatsoever craft he be, shall be found any more in thee; and the sound of a

millstone shall be heard no more at all in thee; And the light of a candle shall shine no more at all in thee; and the voice of the bridegroom and of the bride shall be heard no more at all in thee: for thy merchants were the great men of the earth; for by thy sorceries were all nations deceived. And in her was found the blood of prophets, and of saints, and of all that were slain upon the earth.
(Revelation 18:21-24)

Chapter 13 – Libya's Prophetic Destiny

And say, Thus saith the Lord GOD; Behold, I am against thee, O Gog, the chief prince of Meshech and Tubal: And I will turn thee back, and put hooks into thy jaws, and I will bring thee forth, and all thine army, horses and horsemen, all of them clothed with all sorts of armour, even a great company with bucklers and shields, all of them handling swords: Persia, Ethiopia, and Libya with them; all of them with shield and helmet: Gomer, and all his bands; the house of Togarmah of the north quarters, and all his bands: and many people with thee. Be thou prepared, and prepare for thyself, thou, and all thy company that are assembled unto thee, and be thou a guard unto them.

(Ezekiel 38:3-7)

Libya is in the news lately for obvious reasons. The popular uprising against the Gaddafi terrorist regime, the savagery of Gaddafi himself, and his brutal and very public execution by militia men were put on display for the world to see. Also publicized was the feckless quality of leadership displayed by the Obama administration, the bungled attempt at coalition building, and the debate as to the wisdom, not to mention constitutionality, of American intervention in the first place; all make for an interesting situation. We have since been treated to the brutal spectacle of the post-Gaddafi Libya, a land overrun by the terrorists the West helped empower, who repaid the deed by the brutal torture and murder of an American diplomat.

God has plans for Libya, which are not as fickle as those of the kings of the earth. Libya is slated to go down to destruction as part of a coalition of nations armed and headed up by Russia and Turkey, and including Iran, Sudan/Somalia, and Ethiopia, in a catastrophic war against Israel that will demonstrate to the world that the LORD is the only true God.

It is beyond interesting; it is distressing that the USA is lending its strength to make war on behalf of Al Qaeda, which is leading the opposition to Gaddafi, in the eastern province of Cyrenaica, a long-known hotbed of Islamist fervor. We have aided Al Qaeda before, when we bombed our former allies, the Serbs, into ceding Kosovo to the Albanian branch of Al Qaeda, under the Clinton administration. Elections have consequences, but then again, God is sovereign.

Did you notice that I said the eastern province that is resisting Gaddafi in the name of Al Queda is Cyrenaica? Remember Simon of Cyrene? The man who carried Jesus' cross was from Libya! At one time in the earliest Christian centuries, North Africa was the Christian center of the world. There were several Cyrenians among the first disciples, and at Pentecost.

But Libya has long since been languishing in an Islamic tomb.

In our Ezekiel passage, God says to Russia that He is going to put a hook in his mouth and draw him out, down to the mountains of Israel, for his epic last battle. It is interesting that Vladimir Putin condemned the Obama coalition for its bombing of Gaddafi's strongholds as being a "modern crusade" – words calculated to stir Islamic passions around the world against us.

Persia (Iran) will be part of the coalition bent on destroying Israel. Throughout history, Russia and Persia (Iran) have been bitter enemies. But Russia is now a staunch ally of Iran, her nuclear developer and enabler. Russia plays the devil's advocate for the terrorist state of Iran, resisting any sanctions against her by the world community. Ominously, Russia is also Iran's chief armorer, just as Ezekiel predicted Russia would be: *Be thou prepared, and prepare for thyself, thou, and all thy company that are assembled unto thee, and be thou a guard unto them.* (Ezekiel 38:7)

The expression, *"be thou a guard unto them,"* could as easily be rendered, *"Be thou an armorer unto them."*

Gaddafi was a brutal terrorist. He was not made to pay on this earth for his many brutal crimes, such as the Lockerbie bombing that he ordered, in which a planeload of innocent Western travelers was blown out of the sky. But God sees and remembers. It is important to realize that God is in all of these events, orchestrating all for His glory.

The battle ends poorly for the coalition, all but one sixth are destroyed in the mountains of Israel, for the Holy God takes an attack on Israel personally:

Thus saith the Lord GOD; Art thou he of whom I have spoken in old time by my servants the prophets of Israel, which prophesied in those days many years that I would bring thee against them? And it shall come to pass at the same time when Gog shall come against the land of Israel, saith the Lord GOD, that my fury shall come up in my face. For in my jealousy and in the fire of my wrath have I spoken, Surely in that day there shall be a great shaking in the land of Israel. (Ezekiel 38:17-19)

All of the classic elements of Old Testament warfare by God against pagan invaders come into play. Lightening, thunder and hail, as well as the spectacle of the anti-Israel coalition armies turning on each other in murderous confusion. The divine goal is that all of the earth will know, and perhaps most importantly, Israel will again know that there is a living God, and the LORD is He.

And I will call for a sword against him throughout all my mountains, saith the Lord GOD: every man's sword shall be against his brother. And I will plead against him with pestilence and with blood; and I will rain upon him, and upon his bands, and upon the many people that are with him, an overflowing rain, and great hailstones, fire, and brimstone. Thus will I magnify myself, and sanctify myself; and I will be known in the eyes of many nations, and they shall know that I am the LORD. (Ezekiel 38:21-23)

66

Chapter 14 – Gaza: The Nation not Desired

Gather yourselves together, yea, gather together, O nation not desired; Before the decree bring forth, before the day pass as the chaff, before the fierce anger of the LORD come upon you, before the day of the LORD's anger come upon you. Seek ye the LORD, all ye meek of the earth, which have wrought his judgment; seek righteousness, seek meekness: it may be ye shall be hid in the day of the LORD's anger. For Gaza shall be forsaken, and Ashkelon a desolation: they shall drive out Ashdod at the noon day, and Ekron shall be rooted up. Woe unto the inhabitants of the sea coast, the nation of the Cherethites! the word of the LORD is against you; O Canaan, the land of the Philistines, I will even destroy thee, that there shall be no inhabitant. And the sea coast shall be dwellings and cottages for shepherds, and folds for flocks.
(Zephaniah 2:1-5)

The eyes of the world were riveted upon two events in late August of 2005. On August 22, the Gaza eviction was accomplished, in which the government of Israel, pressured by the United States, forcibly removed the remaining Jewish presence in the Gaza strip and in four settlements of the West Bank. In some cases, bodies were disinterred from graves to be reburied in Israeli occupied land.

The world watched a self-imposed Jewish exile over the tearful protests of Jewish home and business owners, to make room for a Palestinian state as dictated by the U.N. Thriving businesses were left behind only to be completely trashed by the Palestinian occupants of the vacated towns and cities, as were the remaining Jewish cemeteries. Many of the Jewish families forced to depart from the land God gave to Abraham, Isaac and Jacob (Gaza was designated to the tribe of Judah), actually disinterred their own dead for fear of desecration. This proved to be prudent, for in the savage celebration after the Gaza evacuation, Palestinians did indeed desecrate Jewish graves! Gaza is now being used as a staging area for rocket attacks on the rest of Israel.

One week to the day later, August 29, 2005, hurricane Katrina made landfall on America's Gulf coast, rendering tens of thousands of Americans homeless, and the flood forcefully disinterred bodies out of American cemeteries. Katrina wreaked havoc on the presidency of George Bush, that up to then, was considered successful.

Although the U.N., the European Union, the United States government and Russia all insist on the creation of a Palestinian state in the midst of the Holy Land that God gave to the seed of Abraham, Isaac and Jacob, the God of the Bible doesn't desire one.

Could the Gaza/West Bank artificially imposed "Palestinian state" be the "nation not desired" in Zephaniah? Commentaries say no. For the most part, they claim that the "nation not desired" is Judah, but the Hebrew word for nation, in the Zephaniah passage, is e-Gui, the word transliterated as Goy, that is the word "gentile," "heathen," or "nation."

The Word of God has something to say about the future of Gaza, the nation currently run by a popularly elected terrorist group, Hamas, and the focal point of the world's attempt to divide the Holy Land into a "two state solution" to the Middle East conflict. Gaza has been designated by the U.N. as part of the homeland of the new Palestinian state. So also has the so-called "West Bank" of the Jordan River, biblically called Judea and Samaria. Since the Israeli Government has forced the Jews who lived and traded there to leave, Gaza has been turned into a complete terrorist enclave, a staging place for terror raids, a persecutor of Jews and Christians.

Gaza was recently in the news for the grisly street celebration held in the streets of her towns after an armed terror cell broke into a Jewish settler home in the West Bank and slit the throats of the Fogel Family: a father, an eleven year old boy, a three-year old and an infant as they slept in their own beds. They then surprised the family's mother as she emerged from the bathroom, and murdered her in cold blood.

The response? Wild celebrations in the streets, passing out sweets and candies to neighbors, prayers and gunfire, a festive celebration! What sane nation would celebrate such atrocities? I can't emphasize this event enough, as it is truly demonstrative of the character of this "nation."

Zechariah tells us that the celebration will one day be turned to agonizing fear for Gaza, after something happens to Syria and to southern Lebanon, in the day when all eyes of men are turned to the LORD:

The burden of the word of the LORD in the land of Hadrach, and Damascus shall be the rest thereof: when the eyes of man, as of all the tribes of Israel, shall be toward the LORD. And Hamath also shall border thereby; Tyrus, and Zidon, though it be very wise. And Tyrus did build herself a strong hold, and heaped up silver as the dust, and fine gold as the mire of the streets. Behold, the LORD will cast her out, and he will smite her power in the sea; and she shall be devoured with fire. Ashkelon shall see it, and fear; Gaza also shall see it, and be very sorrowful, and Ekron; for her expectation shall be ashamed; and the king shall perish from Gaza, and Ashkelon shall not be inhabited. (Zechariah 9:1-5)

Something happens to Syria, particularly Damascus, which terrifies the hopes of Gaza, turning her citizens into streams of refugees. It involves southern Lebanon as well, which today is the stronghold of the Hezbollah terror group, and is also being used as a staging ground to rain rockets upon Israel.

There is no future for a Palestinian state in Gaza or for the "West Bank," in spite of the world's desire. The world will soon see that the only desire that matters is that of the God of the Bible.

Chapter 15 – The West Bank:
Judea and Samaria

Also, thou son of man, prophesy unto the mountains of Israel, and say, Ye mountains of Israel, hear the word of the LORD: Thus saith the Lord GOD; Because the enemy hath said against you, Aha, even the ancient high places are ours in possession. (Ezekiel 36:1-2)

There is a growing controversy between the leaders of the world and the God of the Bible over a particular piece of real estate. The property in dispute is called by the world the West Bank, or at times, "the Occupied Territory" or the Palestinian Authority.

They claim the ancient High places as their own possession...

The United Nations has designated this chunk out of the east side of the state of Israel, along with Gaza, which is a smaller chunk out of the west side of Israel, to be a new Palestinian state. But the God of the Bible refers to it by another name: Judea, Samaria, and also "the mountains of Israel."

The effort is currently underway to lessen the influence of the approximate 600,000 Jewish settlers who have bought land there, irrigated it, and built little hilltop towns in the very heart of Biblical Israel. These settlers are seen as an obstacle to peace in the region, "occupying" land that is earmarked by the world community for the "Palestinian state."

The Obama administration's official policy is that a "no natural growth policy" should be enforced upon the settlers in the West Bank. That means that a Jewish population number should be agreed upon and enforced. In practice, one Obama adviser stated that, "If a Jewish baby is born in the morning, by evening another Jew should be moving out!"

Here is an excerpt from an *AL Monitor* article:

"Secretary of State Hillary Rodham Clinton set the aggressive tone for this initiative in May 2009 when she said, '[President Obama] wants to see a stop to settlements - not some settlements, not outposts, not natural growth exceptions. That is our position. That is what we have communicated very clearly.'" (*AL-Monitor.com* "Israel Parties Merger Thwarts US Push To Halt Settlements," Geoffrey Aronson)

Here also from a blog, the *Israel Insider* quotes US Special envoy George Mitchell:

Israel Insider "Mitchell: Jews in Judea Must Stop Having Babies"

George Mitchell said the United States continues to demand that Israel halt "natural growth" of settlements. And that doesn't just mean no new houses, apartments, schools or kindergartens. That means no new babies.

In a press briefing Tuesday at the State Department, the Obama administration's special envoy to the Middle East called "highly inaccurate" an Israeli newspaper report that the Obama administration would allow "natural growth" of settlements. Mitchell, of Lebanese Arab ancestry, emphasized there has been "no change in our policy."

When asked for a definition of what the term "natural growth" means, Mitchell was unclear — first saying there was no accepted definition, then stating that "the most common definition" is "number of births."

"Well, of course, one of the issues is that there is no universally used and accepted definition," he said, according to a transcript. "The most common definition is by the number of births, but there are many variations of that. I've had numerous discussions with many Israeli and other officials, and there are almost as many definitions as there are people speaking. But I think the most commonly used measure is the number of births."

Mitchell declined to elaborate further when ask a follow-up question. It is unclear whether the American prohibition on Jewish births in Judea and Samaria will also extend to sexual relations. Unclear too is whether the US will follow the Herod and Pharaoh precedents and favor eliminating Jewish newborns as well.

The God of the Bible has other plans for the region, however. He calls this land by different names, i.e., "the mountains of Israel," "Judah," and "Samaria." God dedicated a whole chapter to this area in Ezekiel, offering His perspective on the current controversy. It is startling to read Ezekiel 36 in the light of today's events.

Therefore prophesy and say, Thus saith the Lord GOD; Because they have made you desolate, and swallowed you up on every side, that ye might be a possession unto the residue of the heathen, and ye are taken up in the lips of talkers, and are an infamy of the people: (v 3)

"They have made you desolate..." Judea and Samaria were at one time a well-watered, forested, verdant, *"Land flowing with milk and honey,"* but it has been made desolate in the years since. One way they made her desolate was that, in the time of the 400-year Ottoman rule over the Holy Land, the Turkish governors imposed a tax on trees. The few Arabs that did live there cut down as many trees as possible to avoid the tax, thus turning a once prosperous area into an arid desert.

You are taken up in the lips of the talkers... About one-third of the time at the UN is spent in discussions of the status of Jerusalem, the proposed Palestinian homeland, the problem of the Jewish settlers, the "Two-state Solution" and its obstacles, as if Judea and Samaria have nothing at all to do with the nation of Israel.

• *...That you might be the possession of the rest of the Heathen (nations)...* The U.N. and its supporters are actually treating the land God gave to Abraham, Isaac and Jacob as if it were the U.N.'s to dispose of at will, to decide who can occupy and who can't.

In the light of scripture, we can only conclude that this is what will bring the judgment of almighty God down upon us, for this land is God's alone to dispose of as He has seen fit. As God himself has said:

The land shall not be sold for ever: for the land is mine, for ye are strangers and sojourners with me. (Leviticus 25:23)

• **...And are an infamy of the people...** The West Bank and its stubborn settlers are getting the same bad name the Rhodesians received in the 1970 by the "world community" or the Serbs in the 1990s.

Even in the face of the recent cowardly massacre of a settler family in their own beds by terrorists, the President of the United States made a moral equivalence, deploring the murders and any "Palestinians who have been killed."

The world knows how to isolate a people, demonize them, lionize their tormentors, ignore indignities and outrages against them, and encourage those who would destroy them that they are somehow "on the right side of history." Just ask the Afrikaners, the Rhodesians and the Serbs!

The future of the West Bank does not belong to the unfortunate "Palestinian" people, in spite of the best efforts of the "Kings of the earth and the rulers thereof...."

*But ye, O mountains of Israel, ye shall shoot forth your branches, **and yield your fruit to my people of Israel**; for they are at hand to come. For, behold, I am for you, and I will turn unto you, and ye shall be tilled and sown:*

And I will multiply men upon you, all the house of Israel, *even all of it: and **the cities shall be inhabited,** and the wastes shall be builded: And I will multiply upon you man and beast; and they shall*

73

increase and bring fruit: and I will settle you after your old estates, and will do better unto you than at your beginnings: and ye shall know that I am the LORD. Yea, I will cause men to walk upon you, **even my people Israel;** *and they shall possess thee, and thou shalt be their inheritance, and thou shalt no more henceforth bereave them of men.* (Ezekiel 36:8-12)

The West Bank of the Jordan River is destined to be inhabited by Jews, lots of them. Note that three times in the above passage the Lord says, "My people Israel." Israel will re-inhabit the ancient cities, such as Bethlehem, Hebron, East Jerusalem, Jericho and Nablus; the heart of biblical Israel will again be Jewish over the objections of the so-called "world body."

Chapter 16 – What Will Happen to Israel's Neighbors?

"And there shall be no more a pricking brier unto the house of Israel, nor any grieving thorn of all that are round about them, that despised them; and they shall know that I am the Lord God." (Ezekiel 28:24)

In view of these studies on the Arab nations in Bible prophecy, we must look at Psalm 83. This is a Psalm that is a prayer of Israel; in fact a desperate prayer to God for help in view of an overwhelming attack by a confederation of Israel's near neighbors, who vow to erase Israel from the map.

Keep not thou silence, O God: hold not thy peace, and be not still, O God. The desperate nation pleads with the LORD not to be silent in the face of this assault, as though there had been a period of silence. The supplicant is pleading with God to behold and to take action, to make a declaration of war!

For, lo, thine enemies make a tumult: and they that hate thee have lifted up the head. Because the enemies of Israel happen also to be enemies of the God of Israel. They make a tumult, raising awareness of their claims, ominously calling for war, for annihilation and destruction. They feel at this point that it is their time, and in their confidence, they lift up their head. They are united as never before (Islam has united this once Balkanized region).

They have taken crafty counsel against thy people, and consulted against thy hidden ones. Much consultation has gone into this particular assault. Evidently, unique circumstances have come together to allow them to believe the previously unthinkable: they really believe their time is come.

They have said, Come, and let us cut them off from being a nation; that the name of Israel may be no more in remembrance. We have all been hearing such ranting from the massed demonstrations of Muslims around the world. This expression could be lifted from any sermon on any given Friday in the Muslim world. Or perhaps it could also have been lifted from the countless textbooks by which the young are poisoned to hate the Jews. Most Arab maps have no name of Israel on them; Arab lobbyists have succeeded in de-legitimizing Israel in the eyes of the world. But at this point in the prayer, the enemy is poised to act; they believe they can do it now!

For they have consulted together with one consent: they are confederate against thee: The tabernacles of Edom, and the Ishmaelites; of Moab, and the Hagarenes;

These make up the super-alliance... **The Tents of Edom...** That is either the refugee camps of the Jordanian Palestinians (as Bill Salus, prophecy teacher, asserts in his book, *Israelestine*), or the Jordanian military. **The Ishmaelites of Moab...** This would be the Arab Muslims of central Jordan; **the Hagarenes** would be Egyptian Arabs.

Gebal, and Ammon, and Amalek; the Philistines with the inhabitants of Tyre. Gebal... is an area north of Beirut, Lebanon; **Amman** is north Jordan. **Amalek** is south of the Dead Sea in the Jordanian desert. Amalek is known for its cowardly warfare against the children of Israel, following the Exodus, and sniping at the weak and tired, at the old and at children. Sounds like modern Islamic terrorists.

Remember what Amalek did to you on the way as you came out of Egypt, how he attacked you on the way, when you were faint and weary, and cut off at your rear all who lagged behind you; and he did not fear God. Therefore when the LORD your God has given you rest from all your enemies round about, in the land which the LORD your God gives you for an inheritance to possess, you shall blot out the remembrance of Amalek from under heaven; you shall not forget." (Deuteronomy 24:17-19)

The Philistines... these are the ones who live in the terrorist state of Gaz;, they are not direct descendants of the original

Philistines, rather they are Arabs who, as of 1967, declared themselves to be a nation disenfranchised by Israel, the Palestinians. **Tyre** would be southern Lebanon, now controlled by a rabid Israel hater named Nassralah, who is the spiritual head of Hezbollah. *Assur also is joined with them: they have holpen the children of Lot. Selah. Assur* are the Arabs who are now known as "Iraqis," Sunni Muslims who have recently been "liberated" by America, but who are destined to join with **the children of Lot,** that is Ammon and Moab, northern and central Jordan. This is the coming Arab invasion; they are already making their tumult, agitating and terrorizing with new-found zeal, partly because of the oil money, partly because of the retreat and collapse of traditional restraints.

Deal with them as you did with Midian, with Sisera, with Jabin, at the brook Kishon, who were destroyed at Endor, who became dung for the field. Treat their great men like Oreb and Zeev, Like Zeba and Zalmuna... cover their faces with shame that they may seek your name O Lord. (Psalm 83:10-14)

Because we believe that the Psalms are the God-given expressions of the hopes, aspirations, prayers and worship of Israel, and Israel's Messiah, we believe that these prayers are as sure to be answered by God as any other promise or prophecy of scripture. *"The Word of the Lord is sure, enduring forever..."* (Psalm 19)

Therefore, the fate of Israel's near neighbors is grim. God himself has inspired the requests of this desperate plea for deliverance and shall surely answer these cries in due time. What would such answers look like?

"Deal with them as you did with Midian, Sisera, as to Jabin at the brook Kishon."

The Psalmist was led to pray for a repeat of the battle recorded in Judges 4 and 5, in which God used women in prominent roles to lead Israel's hosts to destroy an Arab multitude. Deborah, the prophetess, mobilized the ragtag army of Israel after they had suffered twenty years of grinding oppression. She received the Word of the Lord, which was a battle plan to overcome the advantage the Arabs enjoyed in superior armor (900 chariots). They were to be drawn into the swollen, flooded plain of the Kishon brook, thus nullifying the chariot mobility.

Sisera, the Arab commander, fled the battle on foot to save his life and came upon the tent camp of an ally. Jael, the wife of the ally, invited the exhausted Sisera into her tent, seemingly to hide him, and plied him with warm milk. This put him to sleep, enabling her to drive a tent stake through his temple!

When Deborah composed a victory Psalm after the battle, by the Spirit of the Lord, she attributed to Jael the same kind of blessing the angel Gabriel would confer upon Mary one day, "Blessed are you among women." For what? For driving a tent peg through the Arab invaders head! Shadows of the coming "head crusher," the seed of the woman, the Messiah who draws near.

Blessed above women shall Jael the wife of Heber the Kenite be, blessed shall she be above women in the tent. He asked water, and she gave him milk; she brought forth butter in a lordly dish.

She put her hand to the nail, and her right hand to the workmen's hammer; and with the hammer she smote Sisera, she smote off his head, when she had pierced and stricken through his temples.

At her feet he bowed, he fell, he lay down: at her feet he bowed, he fell: where he bowed, there he fell down dead. (Judges 5:24-27)

In Psalm 83, the Psalmist is asking God for a replay of this victory upon the united Arab coalition! What a shame for an Arab to be slain by a woman! How humiliating for one in an honor/shame-based culture to be killed this way! Somehow or other, this will happen to Israel's enemies again in the last days.

There is also an obvious connection with the primal prophecy in this story, for we are told that it is *"the seed of the woman"* who will indeed *"crush the serpent's head!"* Jael is praised in much the same way Mary was when she miraculously conceived the ultimate head crusher:

*Blessed above women shall Jael the wife of Heber be, **blessed shall she be above women** in the tent. He asked water, and she gave him milk, she brought forth butter in a lordly dish. She put her hand to the nail, and her right hand to the workman's hammer, she smote Sisera, she smote off his head, when she had pierced and stricken through his temples"* (Judges 5:24-25)

There is no doubt in my mind that the confederacy forming against Israel is Satanic; it is being called in the name of a false god, a bloodthirsty pagan totalitarian system that seeks to enslave the whole world.

The prayer for Israel is that as Deborah, Barak and Jael were empowered to crush Sisera's serpent head; so also would Israel prevail in the last days.

Make their Nobles like Oreb and Zeev – their princes like Zeba and Zalmuna. (Psalm 83:11)

This is a reference to a later war, also fought to overthrow Arab conquerors. It was in the days when God raised up Gideon to be a judge and a savior for Israel. But first God reduced the army to a mere 300 men. When the "innumerable hosts" of Arabs were utterly routed, they were chased out of the Holy Land and scattered. Their leaders, the Arab princes Oreb and Zeeb, were beheaded.

Of particular interest were the Arab princes Zeba and Zalmuna, who were hunted down, captured and slain by Gideon himself. We are then given the detail that Gideon

"...Took away the crescent shaped ornaments off of their camels necks...." (Judges 8:21)

The crescent moon was the symbol of the pagan god Sin, who later was known as Bel, then Habul, the Nabatean moon god who eventually morphed into Allah. The prayer is specific, *"...Do unto them as you did unto Zeba and Zalmuna...."* The request involves the destruction both of the princes and the symbol of the false religion those princes waged war on behalf of, against God's "hidden ones."

Because the evil confederacy arrogates to itself the land which God gave to Israel, God is asked to *"make them as the stubble before the wind."*

Who said let us take the houses of God for our possession, O My God make them like a wheel... as the stubble before the wind, as the fire burns a wood and as the flame setteth the mountains on fire. (Psalm 83:13-14)

The inspired Psalmist asked that this conflict would not only bring judgment to the Arab confederacy, but that it would set "all of the mountains" on fire (mountains are prophetic symbols of human governments).

The world leaders know full well that the Arab-Israeli conflict has had the potential to set all of the world on a course of war and destruction; this is why the U.N. spends more than a third of its time discussing it.

A horrible destruction is coming to the Arab world, but it shall eventually involve all of the world. In Joel 3, God says He will bring "all nations down to the valley of Jehoshaphat" to plead with them there for parting his land and "casting lots" to determine the fate of his people.

I will also gather all nations, and will bring them down into the valley of Jehoshaphat, and will plead with them there for my people and for my heritage Israel, whom they have scattered among the nations, and parted my land. And they have cast lots for my people; and have given a boy for an harlot, and sold a girl for wine, that they might drink. (Joel 3:2-3)

The answer to these pleadings will provoke a conflict that will eventually lead to the total destruction of Arab capitals, such as Damascus and Amman, and will eventually lead to the near destruction of Jerusalem, setting the whole world on a course of fire and destruction, which will necessitate the return of Jesus himself!

Behold, the day of the LORD cometh, and thy spoil shall be divided in the midst of thee. For I will gather all nations against Jerusalem to battle; and the city shall be taken, and the houses rifled, and the women ravished; and half of the city shall go forth into captivity, and the residue of the people shall not be cut off from the city. Then shall the LORD go forth, and fight against those nations, as when he fought in the day of battle. (Zechariah 14:1-3)

The embattled Israel pleads with her God, the LORD, to utterly shame those who unite against her very existence. Twice she prays that her enemies be shamed. This is interesting because the Arabic Islamic culture is a shame-based society and, as the cartoon fiasco has shown us, there is nothing they fear more than being shamed.

Cover their faces with shame, that they may seek thy name, O Lord, let them be confounded and troubled forever; yea let them be put to shame, and perish ... (Psalm 83:17)

Twice the Psalmist prays that the enemies who attack Israel be shamed, but I see a glimmer of hope even in these grim imprecations. When he prays for them to be shamed the first time, it is that they may seek God's name. In other words, he is praying for their conviction and repentance unto salvation. It is my belief that there are millions trapped in the prison that is Islam who will yet be liberated and saved unto God by Jesus Christ.

But the second prayer that they be shamed has a more ominous ring to it, *"Let them be confounded and troubled forever, let them be put to shame and perish. ... "* For those who are set in their ways, confirmed in the "everlasting hatred," sold out to the glory of the moon god and the promise of 72 virgins, nothing awaits but the terror of *"**everlasting shame and contempt**"* spoken of by Daniel the prophet.

As for the Jews and for the Muslim world, so shall it be for the whole world; the next dreadful war shall force upon all nations a choice; neutrality will not be an option. By this fulfillment of this prophetic word, God is calling all men everywhere to repentance, as

81

is brought out in the last verse of this Psalm, *That men may know that you, whose name is Jahweh are the most high over all the earth.* (Psalm 83:18)

Chapter 17 – Tish B'Av, Israel's Day of Sorrow

How hath the LORD covered the daughter of Zion with a cloud in his anger, and cast down from heaven unto the earth the beauty of Israel, and remembered not his footstool in the day of his anger! The LORD hath swallowed up all the habitations of Jacob, and hath not pitied: he hath thrown down in his wrath the strongholds of the daughter of Judah; he hath brought them down to the ground: he hath polluted the kingdom and the princes thereof. He hath cut off in his fierce anger all the horn of Israel: he hath drawn back his right hand from before the enemy, and he burned against Jacob like a flaming fire, which devoureth round about. He hath bent his bow like an enemy: he stood with his right hand as an adversary, and slew all that were pleasant to the eye in the tabernacle of the daughter of Zion: he poured out his fury like fire. The LORD was as an enemy: he hath swallowed up Israel, he hath swallowed up all her palaces: he hath destroyed his strong holds, and hath increased in the daughter of Judah mourning and lamentation.

(Lamentations 2:1-5)

For all of Israel, a solemn day commences at sundown, Saturday, July 28, until sundown the 29th. It is called Tish B'Av (the ninth of the month of Av) in the Jewish calendar. The day is marked by fasting, mourning and solemn prayers by pious Jews around the world, in commemoration of both the Babylonian destruction of the Temple, in 586 BC, and the Roman destruction of the Temple on the same calendar day in 70 AD. Not only had those two horrors occurred on that day, but there have been many, many other incredibly horribly occurrences which concern the Jewish people on this same calendar day through history.

Incredibly, it was on the ninth of Av that;

- The sages tell us that the ten spies discouraged Israel

from occupying the land God gave them, resulting in the forty years of wandering in the wilderness.

• 586 BC, Nebuchadnezzar fulfilled the prediction of Jeremiah, destroying the Temple in Jerusalem, killing one hundred thousand Jews, and carrying hundreds of thousands of others off into Babylonian captivity.

• 70 AD, Titus fulfilled the predictions of Jesus, surrounding the city of Jerusalem, imposing a siege, and finally, on the day of Tish B'Av, destroying the Temple, not leaving one stone upon another. Two-and-a-half million Jews were killed in this war, by famine, disease, infighting; much of the nation was exiled, and 100,000 Jews sold to Roman slave markets.

• On Tish B'Av, 132 AD, the Bar Cochba revolt was crushed, killing over 100,000 Jews.

• 133 AD, Turnus Rufus plows site of the Temple. The Romans then built on the Holy Site the pagan city of Aelia Capitolina.

• 1095 AD, Tish B'Av of that year was the date Pope Urban II called the first crusade, which resulted in the killing of more than ten thousand Jews and the obliteration of Jewish communities in Germany.

• On Tish B'AV 1290, all Jews were expelled from England, property was confiscated, and killings of Jews occurred.

• In 1492 on the same date, Tish B'Av, all Jews were expelled from Spain by order of the "Holy Order" of the Inquisition. There were forced conversions, family separations, pogroms, and much loss of property.

• In 1914, on Tish B'Av, Britain and Russia declared war on Germany. First World War begins. The First World War led to the Second World War and the Holocaust. Over 400 pogroms immediately following the war in Hungary, Ukraine, Poland and Russia. All but one-third of world Jewry would perish.

• On Tish B'Av 1941, Hermann Göring ordered SS general Reinhard Heydrich to make all the necessary preparations for the Final Solution.

• Tish B'Av saw the 1942 mass deportation of Jews from the Warsaw Ghetto to the Treblinka concentration camp begin.

• On Tish B'Av 1994, the deadly bombing the building of the AMIA (the Jewish community center in Buenos Aires, Argentina) took place, which killed 86 people and wounded some 300 others.

• On Tish B'Av 2003, at the Democratic National Convention, Barak Obama was catapulted from relative obscurity to national fame, after giving a speech which electrified the convention. He would go on to become the most avid anti-Israel president in American history.

There are many, many other calamities that have befallen Israel upon this tragic day. I believe there are several conclusions we can glean from the uncanny circumstances of the day.

Tish B'Av points to the veracity of the Word of God. Moses warned that should Israel break faith with God, they would be scattered across the gentile world:

And the LORD shall scatter thee among all people, from the one end of the earth even unto the other;... And among these nations shalt thou find no ease, neither shall the sole of thy foot have rest: but the LORD shall give thee there a trembling heart, and failing of eyes, and sorrow of mind...

(Deuteronomy 28:64-65)

Our God is faithful in judgment as well as in His promises of mercy. Yet in spite of these terrors and calamities, God in mercy has kept his covenant to keep the Jewish people:

This is what the LORD says, he who appoints the sun to shine by day, who decrees the moon and stars to shine by night, who stirs up the sea so that its waves roar— the LORD Almighty is his name: "Only if these decrees vanish from my sight," declares the LORD, "will Israel ever cease being a nation before me." (Jeremiah 31:34-35)

The sun, moon and stars would have to perish before God will allow the Jewish people to perish!

Our God is a merciful savior, who will again turn His attention to the Jewish people in love and mercy -

"At that time," declares the LORD, *"I will be the God of all the families of Israel, and they will be my people."* This is what the LORD says: *"The people who survive the sword will find favor in the wilderness; I will come to give rest to Israel."* The LORD appeared to us in the past, saying: *"I have loved you with an everlasting love; I have drawn you with unfailing kindness. I will build you up again, and you, Virgin Israel, will be rebuilt. Again you will take up your timbrels and go out to dance with the joyful. Again you will plant vineyards on the hills of Samaria; the farmers will plant them and enjoy their fruit. There will be a day when watchmen cry out on the hills of Ephraim, 'Come, let us go up to Zion, to the LORD our God.'"* (Jeremiah 31:1-6 NASB)

We can see by the signs of the times that the Biblical prophecies are being lined up for fulfillment, and the time spoken of in Psalm 102 has come:

*Thou shalt arise, and have mercy upon Zion: for the time to favour her, yea, the set time, is come. For thy servants take pleasure in her stones, and favour the dust thereof. So the heathen shall fear the name of the LORD, and all the kings of the earth thy glory. **When the LORD shall build up Zion, he shall appear in his glory.** He will regard the prayer of the destitute, and not despise their prayer. This shall be written for the generation to come: and the people which shall be created shall praise the LORD.* (Psalm 102:11-16)

Chapter 18 – The Future of Turkey

The modern nation of Turkey is an important player in the events leading to the Day of the Lord. Though it is a Muslim nation at present, in the earliest centuries of the New Testament church, it was what is now known as the Turkish region that the gospel first flourished beyond the borders of Judea and Samaria.

The apostles took the gospel to what then was referred to as the Roman province of Asia, within decades of the resurrection of Jesus. Paul taught there for two years, as recorded in Acts 19. The original letters of the Apocalypse were addressed to churches in Ephesus, Smyrna, Pergamos, Thyatira, Sardis, Philadelphia and to Laodicea, all in modern-day Turkey.

The epistles to Thessalonica, Galatians, I John, I and II Timothy and Revelation all originally addressed Greek-speaking converts in what is now called Turkey. Eventually, the Roman Emperor Constantine, in the 4th century, built a city on the Dardanelles strait, Constantinople, as the eastern capital of the Roman Empire.

For the next thousand years, the Christianity that Constantine officially legalized became the religion of the Byzantine Empire, which extended over the Middle East, a swath of Eastern Europe and all of Turkey.

But with the rise and expansion of Islam, bit by bit, the Byzantine Empire succumbed to the Muslims over the next eight centuries, slowly and steadily until in 1452, Constantinople collapsed into Muslim hands. The Turkish empire that replaced it eventually morphed into the Ottoman empire, a Sunni Muslim caliphate that held sway for five centuries, but which collapsed as an outcome of World War I, the Turks having been on the losing side.

One of Turkey's post-war leaders was a man named Mustafa

Kemal. He was also known as Attaturk, "Father of Turks," and as a hero of the first World War, who had commanded Turkish forces during the ill-fated British invasion of Gallipoli.

In the aftermath of the war, Attaturk initiated sweeping national reforms, culturally, politically and even religiously, separating the power of the mosque from the state, outlawing religious clothing such as the hijab and other forms of Islamic attire. For more than eighty years, these reforms have remained, allowing Turkey to become a modern secular state, a partner with NATO and to be considered for membership in the European Union.

The fairly recent elections in Turkey brought Turkish Islamist elements to power. Already the former friendship with the United States has weakened and Turkey is distancing herself from Israel. One by one, many of Attaturk's reforms are being reversed as Islam reasserts itself in Turkish society. Turkey's long friendship with the United States and with Israel has cooled, and she has began to assert herself as a regional Muslim power with a first-class military and economy.

The prophets of the Bible have much to say about the future of this non-Arab Islamic people. Meshech, Gomer and "Beth Togarmah" (i.e., the house of Togarmeh) are some of the names the Biblical prophets cite when referring to this region.

And the word of the Lord came unto me, saying, Son of man, set thy face against Gog, the land of Magog, the chief prince of Meshech and Tubal, and prophesy against him, And say, Thus saith the Lord God; Behold, I am against thee, O Gog, the chief prince of Meshech and Tubal: And I will turn thee back, and put hooks into thy jaws, and I will bring thee forth, and all thine army, horses and horsemen, all of them clothed with all sorts of armour, even a great company with bucklers and shields, all of them handling swords: Persia, Ethiopia, and Libya with them; all of them with shield and helmet: Gomer, and all his bands; the house of Togarmah of the north quarters, and all his bands: and many people with thee.
(Ezekiel 38:1-6)

Gog, and Magog – Gog is a person, a designation for an anti-God leader of a rebellion. Magog is the name of a region, particularly the southern steppes of Russia, Turkmenistan, Kazakhstan, Tajikistan, Uzbekistan and Azerbaijan.

Meshech and Tubal - Meshech was the son of Japheth, Noah's son. Many believe that Meshech is Moscow, but it has been pointed out in Walid Shoebat's valuable book, *God's War On Terror,* that ancient historians such as Herodotus and Josephus, associate Meshech with the Cappadocians. Cappadocia is a region in Turkey. Tubal was a regional ally of Meshech.

Gomer - This is a reference to the ancient Kimmerian peoples of central Turkey.

Beth Togarmeh - The house of Togarmeh, which was a city-state in eastern Turkey, more recently known as Anatolia.

It may be as many surmise that "Gog" is the head of the Russian people, leading these Islamic nations into battle against the Jews. God addresses him personally in Ezekiel, ensuring him of his defeat. The Russians have certainly been an "armorer" unto these nations, as Ezekiel 38:7 literally says:

...Be thou an armorer unto them.

*Be thou prepared, and prepare for thyself, thou, and all thy company that are assembled unto thee, and **be thou a guard unto them**.*

Though the Turks have traditionally been inveterate foes of the Russians for centuries and were aligned with the US in the cold war confrontation with the Soviet Union, the combination of being refused admission to the EU and the election to office of the Islamist politicians, Turkey has been pursuing deeper ties with the Arab world and with the Russians who are arming it.

After many days thou shalt be visited: in the latter years thou shalt come into the land that is brought back from the sword, and is gathered out of many people, against the mountains of Israel, which have been always waste: but it is brought forth out of the nations, and they shall dwell safely all of them.

Ezekiel tells us that Turkey is slated to participate in a multinational invasion of Israel, which is doomed to suffer a direct judgment of God as a consequence, and on the basis of Genesis 12:3, "*...I will bless those who bless you and curse those who curse you.*"

The Turks will be there for the terrible war, with their "grade A" military, Western trained and equipped. They will come down, along with the Turkik nations of the former Soviet Union, as well as with the coalition consisting of Iran, Libya, Somalia/Sudan, and possibly led by Russia. All of these nations are united in a bitter hatred of Israel, and all except Russia have Islam in common, to stoke that hatred.

They will serve as a living and dying demonstration that there is truly a God in the earth, as prophesied by Ezekiel and others:

Therefore, thou son of man, prophesy against Gog, and say, Thus saith the Lord God; Behold, I am against thee, O Gog, the chief prince of Meshech and Tubal: And I will turn thee back, and leave but the sixth part of thee, and will cause thee to come up from the north parts, and will bring thee upon the mountains of Israel: And I will smite thy bow out of thy left hand, and will cause thine arrows to fall out of thy right hand. Thou shalt fall upon the mountains of Israel, thou, and all thy bands, and the people that is with thee: I will give thee unto the ravenous birds of every sort, and to the beasts of the field to be devoured. Thou shalt fall upon the open field: for I have spoken it, saith the Lord God. And I will send a fire on Magog, and among them that dwell carelessly in the isles: and they shall know that I am the Lord. So will I make my holy name known in the midst of my people Israel; and I will not let them pollute my holy name any more: and the heathen shall know that I am the Lord, the Holy One in Israel. (Ezekiel 39:1-7)

Chapter 19 – Iran's Demon Possession

*And said, O man greatly beloved, fear not: peace be unto thee, be strong, yea, be strong. And when he had spoken unto me, I was strengthened, and said, Let my lord speak; for thou hast strengthened me. Then said he, Knowest thou wherefore I come unto thee? and now will I return to fight with **the prince of Persia:** and when I am gone forth, lo, the prince of Grecia shall come. But I will shew thee that which is noted in the scripture of truth: and there is none that holdeth with me in these things, but Michael your prince. (Daniel 10:19-21)*

*And the sixth angel poured out his vial upon the great river Euphrates; and the water thereof was dried up, that the way of the kings of the east might be prepared. And I saw three unclean spirits like frogs come out of the mouth of the dragon, and out of the mouth of the beast, and out of the mouth of the false prophet. **For they are the spirits of devils, working miracles, which go forth unto the kings of the earth and of the whole world, to gather them to the battle of that great day of God Almighty.** (Revelation 16:12-14)*

The Persians are heirs of one of the great world civilizations. Mighty kings and rulers such as Cyrus the great, Darius and Xerxes once ruled a vast empire, from India to Ethiopia and including the land of Israel. Daniel predicted that the Persians would be the second of four pagan world empires to rule over the chosen people, and lived to see the day that Persia overcame Babylon to rule the known world.

The Persian conquerors were benevolent towards the Jews, releasing them from captivity in Babylon, sending any who would go, back to their land, financing the rebuilding of the temple and of Jerusalem, as Isaiah had foretold hundreds of years beforehand, even naming the Persian king who would do so, i.e., Cyrus.

That confirmeth the word of his servant, and performeth the counsel of his messengers; that saith to Jerusalem, Thou shalt be inhabited; and to the cities of Judah, Ye shall be built, and I will raise up the decayed places thereof: That saith to the deep, Be dry, and I will dry up thy rivers: **That saith of Cyrus, He is my shepherd, and shall perform all my pleasure: even saying to Jerusalem, Thou shalt be built; and to the temple, Thy foundation shall be laid.** (Isaiah 44:26-28)

Persia eventually threw off the Greek rulers who succeeded Alexander and remained independent and resistant to the Roman Empire that followed. Persian culture developed over the centuries around the religion of Zoroaster.

For our purposes, we pass over Persian history to the Islamic conquest of the entire Euphrates basin in 636 AD. The ancient civilizations of Persia and Mesopotamia (Iraq), which for centuries remained successful in their resistance to Roman aggression, were rapidly swallowed up in Islamic invasions. They have both been embalmed and buried in an Islamic grave to this day. Strict religious subjugation of these ancient people have been the rule ever since.

It is important to note at this point that Persia adopted the Shiite version of Islam as opposed to the Sunni version that most of the Arab Muslim world subscribes to. This significant rift within Islam stems from the death of Mohammed and the debate about who should be his successor.

However, for a brief time in the recent past, Persia underwent a brief "Westernization" process as a result of being with the allies in World War II. Shortly before the war, Persia was renamed Iran to emphasize her Aryan identity. After the war, the US was allowed to work with Iran to develop their oil industry.

When the Shah of Iran began an aggressive modernization campaign in the 1960s -70s, the Mullahs (Shiite Clergy) revolted. One of the most vocal critics of the Shah's secularizing and democratic reforms was an exiled Iranian cleric, the Ayatollah Ruhollah Khomeini. His use of cassette sermons, which smuggled into Iran in the hundreds of thousands, radicalized and

92

inflamed the Iranian population against the Shah.

Furthermore, US president Jimmy Carter, for whom the centerpiece of his foreign policy was human rights, could not countenance the Shah's violent suppression of the increasing revolt. As reports of "human rights" abuses poured out of Iran, the Carter administration distanced itself further from the Shah, until in 1979, the Shah and his family fled Iran.

When the Ayatollah Khomeini emerged from exile, landing in Tehran, hundreds of thousands of fanatical Shiites thronged to get a glimpse of the man who had come to lead the world's first modern Islamist revolution. Iran was plunged into a Shiite, theocratic nightmare from which she has not yet recovered. Sharia law has been written into a new Iranian constitution, and human rights abuses that Carter couldn't have fathomed have become commonplace in Iran. Millions of Persians have been arrested, tortured and killed at the hands of the Islamic revolution.

This one-time advanced, Western-friendly nation in the Middle East has become the inveterate enemy of the US and of Israel, exporter of global terror, and the model for the radical Islamist movement around the globe. The blood that is on the Mullahs' hands since 1979 cries out against them.

It is as though an evil spirit has animated and taken possession of this ancient nation. Everywhere in Iran, almost overnight, the frowning face of Khomeini glowered from bill boards, placards and signs. Religious police squads appeared on the streets, rebuking, admonishing, even beating and arresting any who seemed too "Western" or any females who were unaccompanied by relatives or improperly clothed. Women who recently had been dressed and made up in up-to-date fashion were now entombed in the ever-present black chador.

Indeed there is an evil spirit, a fallen "prince," the Prince of Persia described in Daniel chapter ten. Since 1979, this evil spirit seems to have been released into Iran and has been given free rein to suppress Iran, crush any dissenters, and to entomb the once modern nation in a rabid expression of Islam, making Iran a base for the violent expansion of Islam through terror.

Iran's leaders routinely vow to "wipe out Israel" and to destroy the "great Satan," as they arm themselves with nuclear weapons in spite of Western objections. The Iranian president, Ahmadinejad, really believes he is in communication with the 12th Imam, the Mahdi, who lives in the bottom of a well and who will emerge for the apocalypse of the last day. Here from an article by Charles Krauthammer, *Is Iran Arming For Armageddon*?

"Like Judaism and Christianity, Shiite Islam has its own version of the messianic return – the reappearance of the Twelfth Imam. The more devout believers in Iran pray at the Jamkaran mosque, which houses a well from which, some believe, he will emerge.

"When Ahmadinejad unexpectedly won the presidential elections, he immediately gave $17 million of government funds to the shrine. Last month Ahmadinejad said publicly that the main mission of the Islamic Revolution is to pave the way for the reappearance of the Twelfth Imam."

An aspect of the way God will judge the nations is by removing their right minds from them; we are told in the second Psalm, that *the heathen rage and the people imagine a vain thing.*

Iran is a prime example that truly "evil spirits" are driving the nations of the world towards Armageddon.

Pray for the people of Iran, many of whom would love to be able to receive the salvation that is in Jesus. Even in judgment God shows mercy.

On a recent trip to the UK, in three separate cities, I met lovely Persian young people who had all testified of dreams and visions that eventually led them out of Islam into the gospel message of the grace of God and eternal life in Christ.

Chapter 20 – This is Their Hour and the Power of Darkness

Then Jesus said unto the chief priests, and captains of the temple, and the elders, which were come to him, Be ye come out, as against a thief, with swords and staves? When I was daily with you in the temple, ye stretched forth no hands against me: but this is your hour, and the power of darkness. (Luke 22:53)

The ordeal of our Savior in his trial and crucifixion are recapitulated in the last days of this present evil age. It seemed as though evil had triumphed and with impunity was boasting in the defeat of all goodness. Where was God when corrupt high priests and scribes falsely accused Jesus and brutally abused him?

This is the situation we face today. It seems that evil and vice have prevailed, and that no good deed goes unpunished. Evil parades itself, it taunts the righteous, gloating in its apparent victory over all that was at one time considered good and decent.

For example, there has never been a better time to be a Mohammedan. The followers of the depraved brigand seem to be advancing every single day into the former "Christian" world. Even after 9-11 and the 12,000 atrocities since then visited upon the West in the name of Allah, Islam has not had to answer for its murderous legacy, due to a "perfect storm" of circumstances.

It so happens that the West is in a state of civilizational paralysis, having forsaken the "cultural" part of its culture, i.e., Christianity. The intellectual "elites" over the last century have led in a rebellion against the religion that made the Judeo-Christian West the greatest civilization in history.

We don't have the will to absolutely and resolutely defend our own civilization, having bought into the philosophy of atheists and degenerates. Liberty and the rule of law were ideals that Western people would die on the battlefield to defend, or even to liberate others to enjoy. We were not all Christians, of course, but we operated out of a Judeo-Christian ethos, willing to sacrifice blood and treasure to save others. But who would want to shed one drop of blood for the obvious lie that is multi-culturalism? Who would die so that homosexuality could be freely expressed anywhere in the world? Why would we fight to defend the "gains" of the disaster that was the sexual revolution?

Everywhere in Europe and America, our "secular elite" leadership so despise our own civilization that they promote and exalt anything, even murderous and barbaric Islam, rather than our own Judeo-Christian culture that has brought such light and benefit to so many. Through immigration and abortion and birth control, they seem to be trying to neutralize and cancel out the civilization that once was.

Truly the Psalmist is right, *"the Kings of the earth and their rulers take counsel together against the Lord and His Messiah!"*

The Muslim world is licking its chops; this is their time, seemingly. Like an opportunistic disease, Islam feeds on the decaying body politic of the West and makes gains unheard of in the long 1,400-year struggle against the Christian world. If there were a modern Charles Martel or a Jan Sobieski to arise, no doubt "world governing" bodies, such as the U.N., would immediately move to castrate and hogtie them, perhaps even bringing charges against them for "hurting Muslim feelings."

Furthermore, there has never been a better time to be a sodomite. From being universally reviled for their utterly degrading and unhealthy practices, sodomites are the current "Civil Rights" victims of the post-Christian and post-modern world. Now they are regarded as good, and those who hold to the long-established and immensely successful institution of marriage are regarded as evil. This inversion of values that Isaiah warned us of is upon us, for *"woe to those who call good evil and evil good!"*

This inversion has come about because of a confluence of forces: television, the inability of the west to combat pornography, the departure from faith, false guilt about Civil Rights and confusion and disenfranchisement of the former social order. Also, a very sophisticated marketing of evil, which has taken on the challenge of making the repulsive and unhealthy seem good and wholesome!

It seems now that everywhere we turn, those who *"sigh and cry for the abominations done in the land"* are compelled to witness the seeming victory of the sodomite. The ultimate "punch in the gut" is the desecration of the U.S. military by homosexuals. We now must undergo the media "celebration" of the first openly homosexual (I refuse to use the word "gay" for that is a lie!) Army general, a lesbian.

The US military has always been fastidiously apolitical, being the army of a Democratic Republic, an army of "we the people." There were regulations against soldiers wearing the uniform in the service of any political or factional event. However, those regulations were waived so that homosexuals could wear the uniform to "gay pride" events!

These advances have been rapid and demoralizing for those who love Judeo-Christian America, Britain and Europe. There are many shepherds and guardians who are succumbing to the pressure to acquiesce to evil, not necessarily in deed, but in word. Islam and homosexuality are two of the new "sanctities" that we are supposed to agree to, if not praise out right.

It is one thing to be lied to constantly, but we are beyond that. Now the pressure is on to force those of us who resist this evil to repeat these lies, or at least outwardly to agree with them (to the loss of our soul). We must remember in this dark time of the apparent triumph of evil, the words of Jesus, when he looked evil in the face and proclaimed the sovereignty of the Holy God. The infinitely righteous judge of all of the earth is taking names and preparing to come in Holy vengeance.

And to you who are troubled rest with us, when the Lord Jesus shall be revealed from heaven with his mighty angels, In flaming fire taking vengeance on them that know not God, and that obey not the gospel of our Lord Jesus Christ: Who shall be punished with everlasting destruction from the presence of the Lord, and from the glory of his power; When he shall come to be glorified in his saints, and to be admired in all them that believe (because our testimony among you was believed) in that day. (2 Thess 1:7-9)

This is your hour. It is given by God to the beast to *"make war with the saints and even overcome them..."* but only for a brief and set time of testing. God is allowing evil to parade in all of its naked deformity to give all men a clear choice before the final judgment falls.

...And the power of darkness... Darkness is not mere ignorance, rather it is the refusal to see and enter into the light. The unsaved people want this; they have insisted upon it, and therefore, for a brief moment, they are allowed to build their Utopia. This has happened because of years of resistance to the Holy Ghost; God is giving our societies up to what they have long clamored for: a godless society *à la* "Imagine" by John Lennon.

God delights in hiding his glory and power in apparent weakness. Remember David, the littlest one of Jesse? Remember the capture of the Ark of God by pagans? How could Philistines be allowed to handle the earthly throne of the LORD and not die instantly, like Uzzah? Remember the cross of Jesus? It seemed then also that all that is holy, good and decent had been profaned and trampled underfoot, but "weeping may endure for the night, but in the morning, shouts of joy!" Maranatha!

Chapter 21 – The Prophetic Relevance of the Story of Balaam

Part One

And the children of Israel set forward, and pitched in the plains of Moab on this side Jordan by Jericho. And Balak the son of Zippor saw all that Israel had done to the Amorites. And Moab was sore afraid of the people, because they were many: and Moab was distressed because of the children of Israel. And Moab said unto the elders of Midian, Now shall this company lick up all that are round about us, as the ox licketh up the grass of the field. And Balak the son of Zippor was king of the Moabites at that time. He sent messengers therefore unto Balaam the son of Beor to Pethor, which is by the river of the land of the children of his people, to call him, saying, Behold, there is a people come out from Egypt: behold, they cover the face of the earth, and they abide over against me: Come now therefore, I pray thee, curse me this people; for they are too mighty for me: peradventure I shall prevail, that we may smite them, and that I may drive them out of the land: for I wot that he whom thou blessest is blessed, and he whom thou cursest is cursed. (Numbers 22:1-6)

It is unfortunate that all too often Bible stories are relegated to Sunday school morality lessons, flannel-graph pictures, Veggie Tales or children's coloring books. This is a shame, because Bible stories are revealed as salvation history, from God and to adults. They are not mere morality tales; they are history. And they are prophecy. They serve to reveal the first and second comings of the Messiah.

The story of Balaam in the book of Numbers is an example of how relevant and prophetic Bible stories really are. The setting is in the Exodus wanderings of Israel, the newly redeemed slave nation, entering into the land God promised them, through Abraham, Isaac and Jacob. They had been in exile from the land, in Egypt for 400 years, but the time had come for them to possess it.

Is that not the position Israel is in today? Having been exiled since 70 AD, Israel has come back to life again and is currently in the process of returning to the land God promised Abraham, Isaac and Jacob.

But there was much consternation among those who dwelt in the land in Israel's absence, particularly Israel's Arab neighbors, the Midianites, Moabites and Ammonites.

Even so today, Israel's Arab neighbors are very concerned about the Jewish State, and continually raise a tumult, whether it be the five major wars, the ongoing terror campaign of the last forty years, or the aggressive use of oil as leverage to force the nations to disinherit Israel.

Balak, one of the Arab/Moabite kings, was particularly frightened of Israel, having seen the destruction wrought upon the stronger Amorite kingdom and upon the kingdom of Og, and had heard of the total devastation of Egypt. This man knew it would be impossible to defeat Israel by military means; he would have to resort to something else to resist them.

Israel's modern return to the land has had a startlingly similar impact upon the neighboring nations of Jordan, Egypt, Arabia, Syria, Yemen, Iraq and Lebanon. Having failed to defeat them in five major wars, in spite of overwhelming superiority of numbers, weapons and wealth, as well as the element of surprise, the humiliated Arabs have had to adapt. They have since united to use oil as leverage. The humiliated Arabs would make Europe and America pay for their support of Israel. Petro-wealth would be wielded strategically to affect the foreign policy of the nations against Israel. This has been successfully achieved over the past forty years.

In the story in Numbers, Balak seeks to hire a diviner to "curse Israel," offering him wealth in exchange for pronunciations of doom, failure and defeat upon Israel. The word "curse" here is a term which means to hollow out, to drain, to empty. He would hire someone to hollow out Israel's confidence, to empty her of inward conviction.

Is this not startlingly modern? Politicians, news anchors, leaders in education and even whole departments in universities have been bought by Arabs. Pop stars, foreign ministers, opinion shapers and molders, and respected mainstream religious leaders now publicly de-legitimize Israel to demoralize her sense of being in the right, to hollow out Israel's conviction to stay the course. Fox News also is now owned in part by a Saudi prince.

Those millions of petrol-dollars have steadily had their effect, eroding the support for Israel since the Six-Day War, glamorizing the "Palestinian cause" and repeating calumny after calumny. World opinion is slowly turning against Israel. There have been boycotts, street demonstrations and even open persecution of Jews in Europe, and the pro-Israel climate in America has cooled rapidly.

The last bastion of support for the state of Israel has been the world of Evangelical Christianity, but now even there, voices are calling for a more pro-Palestinian outlook, in the name of "social justice" combined with replacement theology.

But how will it end? Can Israel really ever successfully be cursed?

And Moab was sore afraid of the people, because they were many: and Moab was distressed because of the children of Israel. And Moab said unto the elders of Midian, Now shall this company lick up all that are round about us, as the ox licketh up the grass of the field. And Balak the son of Zippor was king of the Moabites at that time. He sent messengers therefore unto Balaam the son of Beor to Pethor, which is by the river of the land of the children of his people, to call him, saying, Behold, there is a people come out from Egypt: behold, they cover the face of the earth, and they abide over against me: Come now therefore, I pray thee, curse me this people; for they are too mighty for me: peradventure I shall prevail, that we may smite them, and that I may drive them out of the land: for I wot that he whom thou blessest is blessed, and he whom thou cursest is cursed. And the elders of Moab and the elders of Midian departed with the rewards of divination in their hand; and they came unto Balaam, and spake unto him the words of Balak. (Numbers 22:3-7)

The Midianite king of Moab was frightened. He had heard the story of the Exodus out of Egypt of the children of Israel. The fame of their mighty God had been melting pagan hearts throughout the Canaanite region for forty years. They knew about the plagues, the Red Sea, the miracles of manna, and the defeat of the Amorites, the Amalekites, and of Og, King of Bashan. King Balak felt very threatened by this pilgrim people.

He need not have, though, for God had already instructed Israel, through Moses, to refrain from any attempt to harass or dispossess the Moabites. Had they inquired they would have seen they were in no danger.

And the Lord said unto me, Distress not the Moabites, neither contend with them in battle: for I will not give thee of their land for a possession; because I have given Ar unto the children of Lot for a possession.
(Deuteronomy 2:9)

Ye shall buy meat of them for money, that ye may eat; and ye shall also buy water of them for money, that ye may drink.
(Deuteronomy 2:6)

Had the Moabites, Ammonites and Edomites been accommodating to God's chosen nation, they would have been blessed of God and well compensated by Israel for water, food and any other expenses incurred whilst Israel passed through. But hatred, fear and ignorance of the God of Israel prevented that from happening. So it is today. Israel seeks to pay her way, but her Arab neighbors hate and fear her.

So a delegation was sent to the river Euphrates to retrieve a celebrated *Kasem*, a pagan prophet. Balaam's fame preceded him, for it was a four-hundred-mile journey to fetch him. Such prophets were hired because it was believed that they knew how to negotiate the various national gods, in some cases even turning them against their own people by various sacrifices, conjurations and by specializing in the knowledge of such gods. Balaam made it his business to learn about the gods. He had heard about the LORD God of Israel, though up to this time, he had no dealings with Him.

The message Balak sent to entice Balaam contained a line of flattery that betrayed specific knowledge of the LORD, for he attributed to Balaam a perverse form of the Abrahamic blessing of Genesis 12:3, in which God says to Abraham:

And I will make of thee a great nation, and I will bless thee, and make thy name great; and thou shalt be a blessing: And I will bless them that bless thee, and curse him that curseth thee: and in thee shall all families of the earth be blessed. (Genesis 12:2-3)

Whereas Balak's flattering message to Balaam likened him unto God when it said:

Come now therefore, I pray thee, curse me this people; for they are too mighty for me: peradventure I shall prevail, that we may smite them, and that I may drive them out of the land: for I wot that he whom thou blessest is blessed, and he whom thou cursest is cursed. (Numbers 22:6)

Thus the real meaning of the story of Balaam is the attempt to refute the blessing God gave to Abraham and his seed. "I will bless them who bless you and curse them who curse you…"

Can the Lord ever be persuaded to reverse this curse? We will all see shortly…

Chapter 22 Setting Out to Curse Israel

Balaam - Part Two

...Having eyes full of adultery, and that cannot cease from sin; beguiling unstable souls: an heart they have exercised with covetous practices; cursed children: Which have forsaken the right way, and are gone astray, following the way of Balaam the son of Bosor, who loved the wages of unrighteousness;
(2 Peter 2:14-15)

And the elders of Moab and the elders of Midian departed with the rewards of divination in their hand; and they came unto Balaam, and spake unto him the words of Balak. And he said unto them, Lodge here this night, and I will bring you word again, as the Lord shall speak unto me: and the princes of Moab abode with Balaam. And God came unto Balaam, and said, What men are these with thee? And Balaam said unto God, Balak the son of Zippor, king of Moab, hath sent unto me, saying, Behold, there is a people come out of Egypt, which covereth the face of the earth: come now, curse me them; peradventure I shall be able to overcome them, and drive them out. And God said unto Balaam, Thou shalt not go with them; thou shalt not curse the people: for they are blessed. (Numbers 22:7-12)

We have been saying that the story from the book of Numbers has an amazing relevance for our situation today, as do all of the Bible stories. This account is far more than a moralistic anecdote; rather it is a true history of God's dealings with His chosen people, Israel, and the nations around her.

We also maintain that this story is prophecy. It has to do with what will happen again (and is happening) in the time of the end, in the days when the LORD will fulfill all of His promises to resurrect and restore Israel to her prophesied glory.

104

Once again, Israel is being restored back to the land God gave Abraham, Isaac and Jacob. And once again the nations of the world, especially the Arab neighbors of Israel, are agitated, perplexed and frightened. The return of Israel to her land after nearly two thousand years of exile is considered a miracle by Christians and Jews, but to the Arab/Muslim world, May 14, 1948 is called "al Naqba," the catastrophe. Balak also considered the Exodus of Israel into the land a catastrophe.

Furthermore, we have another starting parallel to our own day, for once again, powerful Arabs are seeking to use wealth to entice people to curse Israel. The Saudis alone have spent millions of dollars to endow departments at major universities, such as Harvard and Georgetown; they have bought into news and publishing concerns as well. Oil-rich Arab princes have purchased the services of lobbyists and politicians, and perhaps most scandalously, they have influenced mainstream churches, all towards the same end: they would disenfranchise, disqualify, and de-legitimize Israel in world opinion.

We now come to another aspect of the modern relevance of Balaam, that of the danger of false prophets. Balaam wasn't a Hebrew prophet; he was a *Kasem*, a pagan seer, one who dealt in the negotiation of national gods. He knew the lore, the demands of the deities, the sacrifices, the controlling phrases, the secret names and pronouncements, and was renowned as one who could flip the allegiances of national gods. Perhaps he could negotiate on Balak's behalf with the LORD of Israel: for a hefty fee, of course.

But when Balaam prayed to the God of Israel, the LORD spoke to him! He told Balaam three things very clearly: two commands and one clear fact:

- You shall not go with this people.
- You shall not curse Israel.
- I have blessed them.

But in the morning, Balaam related only one of these three Words from the LORD to the waiting delegation of Arabs. He heard

God, indeed, but held back two very important aspects of God's word from them, and the one word he did tell them was put in such a way as to indicate that Balaam himself wished it wasn't so.

He only told them only that "the LORD refuses to allow me to go with You."

Why didn't he tell them the truth he knew came from the LORD? He held back because he wanted to leave the door open for more negotiation; perhaps he could keep the Arabs "on the string" to "up the price" while he worked on negotiations with the LORD himself.

We have such a plague today in the church and in Judaism as well. People who have heard from God at one time or other but for their own reasons hold back the full truth of what they know. They believe that as "middle men," they can profit in some way or other by holding back or altering revealed truth.

Many mainline denominational leaders know that the Word of God specifically says that Israel is chosen, but to please the world spirit, which is currently sympathetic with the "Palestinian cause," they acquiesce to divestment movements, denominational condemnations, and take sides against the only real democracy and civilized country in the Middle East. False prophets!

There are other areas where this plague is rife, such as preachers who won't condemn homosexuality, ecumenism, or warn of Hell and the wrath of God. They know it is there in the Word, but it would hurt them personally to get real about it, so, like Balaam, they hold back.

I have heard of rabbis who curse those who study chapter 9 of the book of Daniel because they know that Daniel prophesied the timing of the Messiah, and that he would have had to have come between 30AD and the time of the destruction of the temple in 70AD. Why would servants of the Word of God do this? Because they are really servants of themselves and see God's word as a means to their own end.

Balaam is alive and well.

He knew but held back the two most important parts of the message. He should have told these Arabs that the LORD said, "YOU shall not curse Israel" and also that "God has blessed them." In effect he, like so many modern "clergy," Christian and Jewish alike, was trying to downplay or deny by omission Genesis 12:3, the real meaning of this story.

"And I will make of thee a great nation, and I will bless thee, and make thy name great; and thou shalt be a blessing: And I will bless them that bless thee, and curse him that curseth thee: and in thee shall all families of the earth be blessed" (Genesis 12:2-3)

And Balak sent yet again princes, more, and more honorable than they. And they came to Balaam, and said to him, Thus saith Balak the son of Zippor, Let nothing, I pray thee, hinder thee from coming unto me: For I will promote thee unto very great honor, and I will do whatsoever thou sayest unto me: come therefore, I pray thee, curse me this people. And Balaam answered and said unto the servants of Balak, If Balak would give me his house full of silver and gold, I cannot go beyond the word of the Lord my God, to do less or more. Now therefore, I pray you, tarry ye also here this night, that I may know what the Lord will say unto me more. And God came unto Balaam at night, and said unto him, If the men come to call thee, rise up, and go with them; but yet the word which I shall say unto thee, that shalt thou do. And Balaam rose up in the morning, and saddled his ass, and went with the princes of Moab. And God's anger was kindled because he went: and the angel of the Lord stood in the way for an adversary against him. Now he was riding upon his ass, and his two servants were with him. (Numbers 22:15-22)

Which have forsaken the right way, and are gone astray, following the way of Balaam the son of Bosor, who loved the wages of unrighteousness; But was rebuked for his iniquity: the dumb ass speaking with man's voice forbade the madness of the prophet. (2 Peter 2:15-16)

Balaam thought the God of Israel was no different from the

other "gods of the nations," which he had previously dealt with as a *Kasem*, that is, a paid seer. But in this case, the LORD clearly spoke to the pagan prophet, instructing him not to go along with the delegation from the king of Moab, Balak. Furthermore, he was not to curse Israel. Why not? Because the LORD pronounced them to be blessed.

But Balaam didn't tell the delegation everything the LORD had said. He failed to tell them clearly that God had forbidden Him to curse them, and that God had blessed these people, Israel. All he related was his own reluctant obedience to the LORD's prohibition upon going with them. He wanted to make the trip back with them but couldn't. The LORD wouldn't allow him to.

This left the door open for further negotiations, higher bids, and perhaps bought some time in case he could change the will of the LORD.

Sure enough, another delegation came from Canaan, 400 miles to the Euphrates river, with greater wealth in order to convince Balaam to curse Israel.

It looked like Balaam was resolute when he assured them

If Balak would give me his house full of silver and gold, I cannot go beyond the word of the Lord my God, to do less or more.

However, in the next breath Balaam told them:

Now therefore, I pray you, tarry ye also here this night, that I may know what the Lord will say unto me more.

Praying further about what you already know to be the will of God is the recipe for self-deception. What would there be to pray about? Had God not already spoken clearly? Was the instruction of the LORD open to negotiation?

Yet God allowed him to do what he wanted to do. This permission is not necessarily a blessing, in some cases it is a judgment. Remember that Jesus told Judas, "What you do, do quickly!" Was that a divine sanction? Or was it more akin to the strong delusion God will send to those in the last days who insist on something like an Antichrist, until God sends them one!

Even him, whose coming is after the working of Satan with all power and signs and lying wonders, And with all deceivableness of unrighteousness in them that perish; because they received not the love of the truth, that they might be saved. And for this cause God shall send them strong delusion, that they should believe a lie: That they all might be damned who believed not the truth, but had pleasure in unrighteousness. (2 Thess 2:9-12)

So the Lord allows the willful prophet to do what the LORD had previously and explicitly forbade him to do, *"Go with them... but speak only what I tell you to speak... "*

But Balaam is so eager for the money, the honor and the fame, he rushed eagerly to join the delegation on the long trip back to Canaan. It is this willful eagerness that explains the fact that the Lord's wrath was kindled against the prophet, and that the Lord himself was to be an adversary to him on the way.

So it is with many these days, who have told themselves that what they have insisted on doing all along was in fact the will of God, in spite of the fact that it contradicts the Word. As they rush headlong after their own lusts, they tell themselves they have divine approval for all of it. Like Balaam, these are totally oblivious to the wrath that is on them.

And the ass saw the angel of the Lord standing in the way, and his sword drawn in his hand: and the ass turned aside out of the way, and went into the field: and Balaam smote the ass, to turn her into the way. But the angel of the Lord stood in a path of the vineyards, a wall being on this side, and a wall on that side. And when the ass saw the angel of the Lord, she thrust herself unto the wall, and crushed Balaam's foot against the wall: and he smote her again. And the angel of the Lord went further, and stood in a narrow place, where was no way to turn either to the right hand or to the left. And when the ass saw the angel of the Lord, she fell down under Balaam: and Balaam's anger was kindled, and he smote the ass with a staff. And the Lord opened the mouth of the ass, and she said unto Balaam, What have I done unto thee, that thou hast smitten me these three times? And Balaam said unto the ass, Because thou hast mocked me: I would there were a sword in mine hand, for now would I kill thee. And the ass said unto Balaam, Am not I thine ass, upon which thou hast ridden ever since I was thine unto this day? was I ever wont to do so unto thee? and he said, Nay. Then the Lord opened the eyes of Balaam, and he saw the angel of the Lord standing in the way, and his sword drawn in his hand: and he bowed down his head, and fell flat on his face. (Numbers 22:23-32)

As the international delegation drew nearer to the place where they intended to curse Israel, strange things began to happen. At one point on the road, Balaam's ass turned off the path and strayed out into a field, provoking Balaam to beat it. Further on, the group was hemmed in between two stone walls along either roadside. Balaam's ass veered sharply, grinding Balaam's foot against the wall, hurting it. This time the act was met with a rain of blows from the peeved seer. Finally, at another narrow pass, the ass simply laid down on the road, refusing to move. This time, Balaam struck the ass in a rage with his staff.

It was then that the Lord opened the beast's mouth:

And the Lord opened the mouth of the ass, and she said unto Balaam, What have I done unto thee, that thou hast smitten me these three times? And Balaam said unto the ass, Because thou hast mocked me: I would there were a sword in mine hand, for now would I kill thee. And the ass said unto Balaam, Am not I thine ass, upon which thou hast ridden ever since I was thine unto this day? was I ever wont to do so unto thee? and he said, Nay.

Furthermore, the LORD who opened the ass's mouth also opened the "seer's" eyes to see the mortal danger he was in, but which the ass delivered him from. Had the ass passed on down the road, Balaam would have been smitten by the angel and would have perished forever.

Now Balaam could see what the ass saw all along. Evidently the "seer" couldn't really see as well as the Canaanite delegation thought he could. Furthermore, by this incident the LORD showed

110

the pagan prophet that even an ass could speak the Word God put in his mouth. This should have been a sign to Balaam pointing to the sovereignty of the God he was now "dealing with."

Furthermore, this incident would be a sign to Balak also. As the prophet tried to cajole, curse and strike the ass into doing what would prove to be fatal to himself, even so Balak would attempt to bribe, berate and threaten Balaam to do what would prove to be his own undoing.

We see this story being played out again on the world scene; the leaders of the West have allowed themselves to be led toward destruction under pressure of the Arabs, seeking Israel's demise. As we get closer and closer to that point, unnatural things are occurring; nature itself is "speaking" to whoever has ears to hear. These unprecedented natural disasters in the USA have been shown to be directly connected to initiatives to divide the land of Israel. But like Balaam, our leaders are blind to the danger at the end of this road.

Finally, we can see a powerful spiritual metaphor in this story, for the lowly ass is like the Messiah and His prophets. The prophets have always endured scorn, shame, beatings and even death, because they see something no one else sees and warn of it, i.e., the coming wrath upon the world.

The Messiah is like this lowly ass also, for He was willing to bear the burden for us willful sinners and to take the strokes to save us from the judgment we deserve.

Chapter 23 Balaam's Oracles

Balaam – Part Three

And he went to an high place. And God met Balaam: and he said unto him, I have prepared seven altars, and I have offered upon every altar a bullock and a ram. And the Lord put a word in Balaam's mouth, and said, Return unto Balak, and thus thou shalt speak. And he returned unto him... And he took up his parable, and said, Balak the king of Moab hath brought me from Aram, out of the mountains of the east, saying, Come, curse me Jacob, and come, defy Israel. How shall I curse, whom God hath not cursed? or how shall I defy, whom the Lord hath not defied? For from the top of the rocks I see him, and from the hills I behold him: lo, the people shall dwell alone, and shall not be reckoned among the nations. Who can count the dust of Jacob, and the number of the fourth part of Israel? Let me die the death of the righteous, and let my last end be like his! (Numbers 23:1-11)

Finally, the delegation came from the Euphrates. Balaam had agreed to come with them to see how he could be of service to King Balak. Certainly, the LORD had already forbade him to go with them once, but upon praying a second time, had he not given Balaam permission? Perhaps the LORD, the God of this people, would also relent on the other prohibition – not to curse Israel.

Balaam had done his homework. He knew that Israel's deity required burnt sacrifices of rams and bullocks, and that He favored the number seven.

And Balaam said unto Balak, Build me here seven altars, and prepare me here seven oxen and seven rams. And Balak did as Balaam had spoken;... And Balaam said unto Balak, Stand by thy burnt offering, and I will go: peradventure the Lord will come to meet me: and whatsoever he sheweth me I will tell thee...

The pagan prophet then set out to do what he perceived his

craft required: he went to a high place to seek for auguries, signs and portents about what the intention of this God was for this people. Perhaps he would see a sign or be put into a trance, or have a vision. Who could know how long it would take? The various national gods could be capricious. But he must have been stunned when immediately he was met by the LORD himself, and given the Word to speak to Balak concerning the bleak prospects of successfully cursing Israel.

How can I curse whom God has not cursed? How can I defy whom God has not defied?

It would be the height of arrogance for any frail human being to dare pronounce a curse on anyone, let alone anyone whom God has not cursed. Can Israel be withstood successfully? How? If God is with them who could possibly stand against them?

For from the top of the rocks I see him, and from the hills I behold him: lo, the people shall dwell alone, and shall not be reckoned among the nations.

Who are these people? This recently redeemed slave nation? What are they doing wandering in the harsh desert? How are they sustained? As Balaam looked down on this strange spectacle of a huge camp surrounding a tremendous pillar of cloud, the Word of the Lord revealed that this is a unique people, *"Behold the people shall dwell alone..."*

This is a nation unlike any other, never able to completely integrate into the "community of nations." Even to this day, there can be a RED CROSS and even a RED CRESCENT, but there will never be a RED MAGEN DAVID, because Israel is not allowed to.

Every other nation gets a vote in the U.N. but Israel; all can serve on the U.N. Security Council but she. Every nation on earth picks where its capital city shall be, and the rest of the world observes it, but in the case of Israel, not so. Every American president since Eisenhower has promised to move our embassy to Jerusalem, only to fail to do so. Israel shall not reckoned among the nations, because by God's election, she is unique. Balaam saw this and prophesied of it.

Who can count the dust of Jacob, and the number of the fourth part of Israel?

There will be no obliteration of this nation; she will one day number as the dust, or as "the sands of the sea…" according to the Word given to Abraham (father of a multitude).

Let me die the death of the righteous, and let my last end be like his!

Curse them? Are you kidding? If I (Balaam) could but die the death of this people, I would consider myself fortunate! To be able to die knowing you have been made right with God? This is worth more than all of the treasures and honors paganism could ever confer.

This is the first prophecy of Balaam over Israel. The pagan prophet opened his mouth thinking perhaps he could curse them, after all the LORD had relented about going with them, hadn't he? But instead, Balaam could only bless them, and in the highest terms, by the Spirit of prophecy.

Needless to say, this infuriated the pagan king. What good is a prophet if he doesn't say what you want him to say? What good is a "god" if he can't be manipulated and used for your own ends?

Like the many who follow the false prophets in our day, both Balaam and Balak held to a pagan notion of God. "God" exists for man. It is for man to learn the ways of "God" so that he might harness this power to use for the good of all. I once saw a million selling "Christian book" called *God's Creative Power Can Work For You!* This is always the sign of a false faith system, the idea that God can be manipulated to work "for me."

And Balak said unto Balaam, What hast thou done unto me? I took thee to curse mine enemies, and, behold, thou hast blessed them altogether. And he answered and said, Must I not take heed to speak that which the Lord hath put in my mouth?

Balaam, however, had already seen something of the power, majesty and sovereignty of this God, and knew that he could only say what this God wanted him to say. The ass incident had taught him that this was a God to be afraid of.

But who knows, maybe we can "make it work" from another mountain?

And Balak said unto him, Come, I pray thee, with me unto another place, from whence thou mayest see them: thou shalt see but the utmost part of them, and shalt not see them all: and curse me them from thence. And he brought him into the field of Zophim, to the top of Pisgah, and built seven altars, and offered a bullock and a ram on every altar. And he said unto Balak, Stand here by thy burnt offering, while I meet the Lord yonder. And the Lord met Balaam, and put a word in his mouth, and said, Go again unto Balak, and say thus. And when he came to him, behold, he stood by his burnt offering, and the princes of Moab with him. And Balak said unto him, What hath the Lord spoken? And he took up his parable, and said, Rise up, Balak, and hear; hearken unto me, thou son of Zippor: God is not a man, that he should lie; neither the son of man, that he should repent: hath he said, and shall he not do it? or hath he spoken, and shall he not make it good? Behold, I have received commandment to bless: and he hath blessed; and I cannot reverse it.

He hath not beheld iniquity in Jacob, neither hath he seen perverseness in Israel: the Lord his God is with him, and the shout of a king is among them. God brought them out of Egypt; he hath as it were the strength of an unicorn. Surely there is no enchantment against Jacob, neither is there any divination against Israel: according to this time it shall be said of Jacob and of Israel, What hath God wrought!

Behold, the people shall rise up as a great lion, and lift up himself as a young lion: he shall not lie down until he eat of the prey, and drink the blood of the slain. And Balak said unto Balaam, Neither curse them at all, nor bless them at all. (Numbers 23:13-25)

115

Balaam's first pronouncement over Israel was a disaster as far as Balak, the king of Moab, was concerned. He had spared no effort or expense in setting up the seven altars, and the seven rams and oxen that were offered to the LORD by the pagan seer. But when the prophet finally went forth to "curse Israel," a profound blessing issued forth instead!

Israel is special; she is separate from all of the nations, and destined to number in the millions. It would be impossible for anyone to curse these whom the Lord has not cursed. Curse them? If Balaam could so much as die their death, he would be fortunate! To be able to die the death of those who are "in the right" with God would be the highest blessing possible.

Balak and Balaam, being pagans, thought like pagans. Surely the first effort had failed for a reason. What had they done wrong? Could it be that the prophet was disturbed by the spectacle of the whole camp of Israel before him? Or perhaps because the location they chose with which to curse Israel was inauspicious. Had they stood on the wrong aspect of the mountain or faced in the wrong direction?

So the seer and the king's entourage struck camp to find a better place from which to destroy Israel. From Mount Pisgah, seven altars were again erected, seven rams and oxen again offered to the LORD, and again the prophet went forth to seek a word against Israel.

But sooner than any expected, the seer returned to the waiting king, and in the spirit of prophecy, commanded Balak to arise to hear the word of the LORD.

The first point of this prophecy is the character of the God of Israel. Unlike the pagan gods who could be capricious, Israel's God doesn't lie, nor can His mind be changed. He is a faithful God, who does what He says He will do and whose purpose cannot be altered.

What purpose is He referring to specifically? This is the context for the familiar verse, "God is not a man that He should lie, or the Son of man that He should repent." It has to do with God's stated purpose to bless those who bless the seed of Abraham, and to curse those who curse them. That purpose cannot be altered by Balak, Balaam or any king or prophet!

Then the prophecy addresses the divine justification of Israel. *"He hath not beheld any iniquity in Jacob, neither hath He seen any perverseness in Israel."*

Many times over the centuries, Israel's enemies have taken courage to persecute her from the very public record of her sins. They feel they have received a mandate to wipe her out for the evils Israel has done.

Those pagans who would have spied on the camp of Israel would already have witnessed the "golden calf" incident, a great deal of murmuring and murderous threats by Israel against Moses and Aaron; Korah's rebellion and numerous other incidences of Israel's unfaithfulness.

What does the prophecy mean when it says that "God doesn't see iniquity in Jacob"? Balaam is prophesying that this is a people justified before God. Through the God-appointed sacrifice, this people's sins are covered, atonement has been made, and God's anger against their sin has been propitiated. In this sense, God sees nothing wrong or perverse in them.

Therefore, it would be impossible to successfully work an enchantment against them; no divination could ever work on them. At the center of the camp of Israel was the tabernacle of God himself, overshadowed by day with the cloud of Glory, and by night with a pillar of fire. God himself dwelt in the midst of them, the King of the universe camped among them.

But Balaam's prophecy looked far ahead to the time of the end, when people would utter in astonishment of these people, "What is God doing through them"" In the Last Days, God will make Israel to be like a lion, ferocious and insatiable; she will not be content until she devours and drinks the blood of her enemies. As Zechariah prophesied also centuries later:

117

In that day will I make the governors of Judah like an hearth of fire among the wood, and like a torch of fire in a sheaf; and they shall devour all the people round about, on the right hand and on the left: and Jerusalem shall be inhabited again in her own place, even in Jerusalem. The Lord also shall save the tents of Judah first, that the glory of the house of David and the glory of the inhabitants of Jerusalem do not magnify themselves against Judah. In that day shall the Lord defend the inhabitants of Jerusalem; and he that is feeble among them at that day shall be as David; and the house of David shall be as God, as the angel of the Lord before them. And it shall come to pass in that day, that I will seek to destroy all the nations that come against Jerusalem.

(Zechariah 12:6-9)

Balak, the king of the Moabites had high expectations when he hired the renowned seer from the Euphrates to curse Israel. But in spite of the preparation, the sacrifices, altars, the use of the sacred number seven and the discerned favorable locations, when Balaam stood up to curse Israel, only blessings would come out. Each time, the blessings increased in intensity and in woe upon Israel's foes.

Perhaps they would find success from another location. So the camp was again struck, and the trek was made to Mount Peor, where an auspicious location was found to set up the seven stone altars for the sacrifice of seven bulls and rams each.

But by this time, the seer realized that the God of Israel was not a god that required the seeking of omens or auguries, as he had attempted in the two previous prophecies. This is a God who cannot be manipulated by "prophets" such as himself, but one who reveals Himself on His own terms.

Therefore, by the time of the third prophecy, Balaam just surrendered himself temporarily, as a tool of the Holy Ghost.

And when Balaam saw that it pleased the Lord to bless Israel, he went not, as at other times, to seek for enchantments, but he set his face toward the wilderness. And Balaam lifted up his eyes, and he saw Israel abiding in his tents according to their tribes; and the spirit of God came upon him. (Numbers 23:1-2)

Out came a prophecy of the fruitfulness and ultimate triumph of Israel!

Balaam the son of Beor hath said, and the man whose eyes are open hath said: He hath said, which heard the words of God, which saw the vision of the Almighty, falling into a trance, but having his eyes open: How goodly are thy tents, O Jacob, and thy tabernacles, O Israel! As the valleys are they spread forth, as gardens by the river's side, as the trees of lign aloes which the Lord hath planted, and as cedar trees beside the waters. He shall pour the water out of his buckets, and his seed shall be in many waters, and his king shall be higher than Agag, and his kingdom shall be exalted. God brought him forth out of Egypt; he hath as it were the strength of an unicorn: he shall eat up the nations his enemies, and shall break their bones, and pierce them through with his arrows. He couched, he lay down as a lion, and as a great lion: who shall stir him up? Blessed is he that blesseth thee, and cursed is he that curseth thee. (Numbers 23:4-9)

Balaam surrendered himself temporarily, as a tool of the Holy Ghost.

And when Balaam saw that it pleased the Lord to bless Israel, he went not, as at other times, to seek for enchantments, but he set his face toward the wilderness. And Balaam lifted up his eyes, and he saw Israel abiding in his tents according to their tribes; and the spirit of God came upon him. (Numbers 23:1-2)

The Scripture makes note of the sight of the tents of Israel. From this particular aspect, Balaam would have been seeing the layout of the whole camp of the Holy people. At the center was the Tabernacle, overshadowed by the glory of God in the form of a pillar of cloud and fire.

Projecting from that center, in the four directions of the earth, would have been four straight lines of thousands of rows of tents, three tribes to the north, three to the south, and three each to the east and the west. Balaam would have been looking down upon a huge cross!

His prophecy likened the camp of Israel to a well-ordered, irrigated and fruitful garden. Such are the people whom God has chosen, transplanted and set aside for cultivation by His word and watered by his Spirit!

They would fill the land with fruit, they would flow like swollen streams, sprouting the healing aloes, and nurturing majestic Cedars. The people of Israel would become like an aloe plant, they would grow as a cedar, because of the water source they draw from. Israel would become like a water carrier whose buckets constantly overflow, spilling and making everything green, refreshing everyone, and overflowing in blessing to all. The seed of Israel would be spread throughout all of the waters, blessing the whole world!

All of this blessing is traceable to the salvation purchased by the blood of the Lamb, when He brought this people out of Egypt. This redeemed slave nation would one day be championed by a King far greater than Agag, which was the title for the Amalekite rulers, a title similar to Pharaoh and Caesar. The King Messiah will ultimately prevail over the final Agag, the Antichrist who will stand as the final representative of all gentile opposition to God and His purposes.

To further this point, Balaam prophesied that Israel would be like the unicorn (the aurochs), a great horned, wild ox raging against and trampling all of her enemies, breaking their bones and finishing them off with arrows.

The Spirit likened Israel also to a lion, as in the last prophecy. This time, the lion is lying down, sated, it has triumphed and eaten its fill, but woe to the one who rouses him! It is interesting that this is very similar to the prophecy Jacob gave to his son Judah:

Judah is a lion's whelp: from the prey, my son, thou art gone up: he stooped down, he couched as a lion, and as an old lion; who shall rouse him up? (Genesis 49:9)

Finally, the Spirit reiterates the warning to the fool's errand that Balaam and Balak have undertaken by quoting in part the blessing and cursing of Genesis 12, *Blessed is he that blesseth thee, and cursed is he that curseth thee.*

Oh, that our current crop of rulers and leaders, sheiks, presidents and kings all would take heed and establish this as their own foreign policy! God doesn't lie.

Chapter 24 – What This People Will Do to You in the Last Days

And Balak's anger was kindled against Balaam, and he smote his hands together: and Balak said unto Balaam, I called thee to curse mine enemies, and, behold, thou hast altogether blessed them these three times. Therefore now flee thou to thy place: I thought to promote thee unto great honor; but, lo, the Lord hath kept thee back from honor. And Balaam said unto Balak, Spake I not also to thy messengers which thou sentest unto me, saying, If Balak would give me his house full of silver and gold, I cannot go beyond the commandment of the Lord, to do either good or bad of mine own mind; but what the Lord saith, that will I speak? And now, behold, I go unto my people: come therefore, and I will advertise thee what this people shall do to thy people in the latter days. (Numbers 24: 10-14)

Balak, the king of Moab, is livid! He has gone to great expense to bring in a seer to curse Israel, but in the three attempts to curse them, the prophet could only bless them. To make matters worse, the blessings he uttered over this strange pilgrim nation increased in intensity each time. Israel would be blessed greatly, and her enemies would be utterly crushed.

Humanly speaking, Balaam would have been fortunate to escape the enraged Arab potentate with his life! Balak didn't merely fire him, he ominously warns him to "flee to your place," as though he would have harmed or even killed him.

But Balaam isn't quite through yet. He still remained under the influence of the powerful Spirit of the God of Israel and had one more devastating Word to deliver to the disappointed king. The son of Ishmael would have to listen to the unveiling of the ultimate purpose of God for this people and of the doom of all of their enemies, of which he sat as representative:

And he took up his parable, and said, Balaam the son of Beor hath said, and the man whose eyes are open hath said: He hath said, which heard the words of God, and knew the knowledge of the most High, which saw the vision of the Almighty, falling into a trance, but having his eyes open:

Balaam is not speaking as a typical pagan seer, one seeking auguries, portents or omens to divine the mysteries hidden from mortal men. Balaam here, by the Spirit, speaks as a man to whom God has been pleased to reveal his will, and not on Balaam's own terms or by his craft, but by a sovereign act of the LORD.

I shall see him, but not now: I shall behold him, but not nigh: there shall come a Star out of Jacob, and a Scepter shall rise out of Israel, and shall smite the corners of Moab, and destroy all the children of Sheth.

And Edom shall be a possession, Seir also shall be a possession for his enemies; and Israel shall do valiantly. Out of Jacob shall come he that shall have dominion, and shall destroy him that remaineth of the city.

Balaam saw a person of great authority, a "Star" and a "Scepter" to arise out of Jacob, a mighty world ruler would arise in the future, at the time of the end who would utterly smite Moab and all that Moab represents, i.e., heathendom that hates, fears and resists Israel to the point of seeking her destruction.

We know from subsequent history that the Moabites were subjugated by David and eventually faded away as a people entirely, being amalgamated into the surrounding Arab peoples, and ceased from being a kingdom, as did also Ammon and Edom. But this is a prophecy about what shall transpire in the last days.

The territory once inhabited by Ammon and Moab is now peopled by a bitter and implacable foe of Israel; indeed the whole region round about Israel is peopled by people very much in the character of King Balak, constantly clamoring for Israel's annihilation. Indeed they are the descendants of Ishmael, Midian, Esau, Moab, and Ammon. They are bound together by a religion that proclaims that "the last days will not come until the Muslims wipe out the Jews...." Their hatred for Israel is described in Ezekiel 35 as the "Everlasting Hatred" that God is going to judge.

This prophecy by one of their own, a pagan seer, is a warning that they are fighting against almighty God Himself in seeking to curse Israel, and that it is doomed to utter and eternal failure from the start.

Balaam proclaims that this "Star out of Jacob" will *"destroy the children of Sheth."* Sheth is not a name; it is a description meaning "tumult." *"He will destroy the children of tumult;"* that is, He will crush every rebel, troublemaker, and enemy of Israel and Israel's God!

It is to be noted that the Islamic Arab world has unleashed upon the civilized world a torrent of tumult in the form of terrorism. Terrorism, sanctioned by the Koran, has necessitated security precautions that have cost the world billions of dollars, has engendered many bloody conflicts and has upset the peace in every society on the globe. Truly, these are the "sons of Sheth."

And when he looked on Amalek, he took up his parable, and said, Amalek was the first of the nations; but his latter end shall be that he perish for ever.

The redeemed nation first encountered national resistance against the Amalekites. Balaam saw their end; they would be blotted out forever: death and eternal perdition to all that the Amalekites are and all they stand for. Deuteronomy 25:17-18 tells us that Amalek's mode of operation was terrorism, attacking the weak and sick stragglers. The terrorists who infest this world are doomed to a fiery end by the coming of the Holy God.

And he looked on the Kenites, and took up his parable, and said, Strong is thy dwelling place, and thou puttest thy nest in a rock. Nevertheless the Kenite shall be wasted, until Asshur shall carry thee away captive.

The Kenites were the tribe that would trick Israel into a treaty and become employed as wood hewers and water bearers for them, rather than being wiped out. Their "strong nest" was to become incorporated into Israel. Thus did the Kenites survive until the Babylonian captivity (Asshur), where they were taken away with Judah. Thus, Balaam predicted the Babylonian captivity.

The contrast is meant to be drawn between the Amalekites, whose resistance doomed them, to the Kenites, Canaanites who assimilated into Israel and thus lived.

Balaam saw all of this. He also saw the final, great Tribulation, and he took up his parable, and said:

Alas, who shall live when God doeth this! And ships shall come from the coast of Chittim, and shall afflict Asshur, and shall afflict Eber, and he also shall perish for ever. And Balaam rose up, and went and returned to his place: and Balak also went his way. (Numbers 24:15-25)

Finally, Balaam saw what Daniel saw centuries later, that Israel herself would come under the rule of gentile powers, first of the east (Asshur, Babylon, Persia), but finally and until the end, the West (ships of Kittim: Greece and Rome).

At the end, in the time of the advent of the Star and Scepter, all of Israel's enemies will be utterly destroyed in a time of tribulation so terrible, Balaam cried out:

Alas, who shall live when God doeth this!

Chapter 25 – Balaam's End

Balaam's prophecy to Balak, the king of Moab, is remarkable on many levels. The fact that Balaam wasn't even a believer is an incredible testimony to the sovereignty of God. Truly he makes even *"the wrath of men to praise Him."*

The fact that he was hired by one of the bitter enemies of Israel to curse them makes this a story about Genesis 12:2-3, which was cited several times in this narrative.

And I will make of thee a great nation, and I will bless thee, and make thy name great; and thou shalt be a blessing: And I will bless them that bless thee, and curse him that curseth thee: and in thee shall all families of the earth be blessed. (Genesis 12:2-3)

Sometimes the blessing was cited perversely, as when Balak applied it to Balaam himself, putting him in the place of God, as the one with the power and prerogative to "bless and curse," but at other times, it was cited in the Spirit of God, as in the third prophecy.

The point could not be more relevant to our own times, as the nations of the world are uniting in their hatred and condemnation of Israel. The heathens rage and the people truly imagine a vain thing when they vainly imagine they can curse Israel and end up intact.

I believe that this story is also important for the incredible scope of the prophecy given to the pagan seer. Balaam, like Moses and Daniel, prophesied the entire course of the chosen nation, as well as the fate of her open enemies until the end of time.

• **The Separation of Israel** – "Lo a people dwelling alone, and not reckoning itself among the nations." Truly in spite of its best efforts, Israel has never been able to integrate fully into the community of nations. Though her backslidden aspiration from the book of Judges was always to be a nation "like other nations," God has separated her for himself.

Even in our own "enlightened times," Israel is treated as a pariah, unable to have a vote in the U.N., unable to name her own capital, Jerusalem. She yet remains unable to sit on the U.N. Security Council and has always been unable to fully integrate into the European nations where she was driven. Truly this is a nation dwelling alone.

• **The Messiah** - "I see him, but not yet." Balaam prophesied the advent of the "Star" out of Jacob, the "Scepter" from Israel, a powerful world ruler who would be given the dominion over all other nations and who would oversee the total destruction of all of those haters of Israel of whom Balak stood as representative and type.

The second-century Jewish pretender, Simon Bar Cochba, the "Son of the Star," was believed to be the fulfillment of this prophecy, until his rebellion destroyed the nation and ended in national dissolution and slavery.

The Star, King Messiah, will be "higher than Agag," which was the title of the then reigning Caananite kings, who like the pharaohs, caesars, emperors and dictators who would follow, all typify the final Agag, the Antichrist.

• **The Babylonian and Persian Captivity of Israel** - Balaam prophesied of the Kenites, a servant tribe who amalgamated with Israel, that they would remain until "Asshur will lead thee away" - Asshur comprised the Eastern kingdoms now known as Iraq and Persia.

• **The Final Western Dominance** – Balaam saw the arrival of the ships of Kittim. How was he to know that Israel would one day so defect from God that she would be turned over to domination by various gentile powers, the first two Eastern (Asshur), and the final two Western (Greece and Rome)?

• **The Great Tribulation** – Balaam saw the destruction of the great cities of the Middle East and the terrible doom of Israel's sworn enemies, calling them the "Sons of Sheth," that is, "children of tumult." Balaam virtually echoes the Savior's warning that unless he returns, "all flesh might perish," when he proclaimed, "Who shall live when God does this?"

Thus the pagan prophet's utterances are comparable to Daniel in scope. God used him in spite of himself, and his prophecies are more sure now than ever. However, in spite of all of this experience, Balaam yet wanted a shot at the money and fame Balak had offered him.

Nevertheless I have a few things against you, for you have there those who hold to the doctrine of Balaam, who taught Balak to put a stumbling block before the children of Israel, to eat things sacrificed to idols and to commit fornication... (Rev 2:14)

By the end of the fourth "parable" of Balaam, both he and Balak the king were fully aware of God's purposes for Israel. The utter impossibility of using any kind of divination against Israel was now obvious to the badly shaken king and to the seer also – whose eyes God had opened.

They would go their separate ways, although the prophet Micah records an exchange between the two of them – Balak inquiring in utter fear and trembling, "What would it take to appease this fearful God?" Balaam's inspired reply would become one of those much-loved verses that few realize the context of.

My people, remember what Balak King of Moab counseled and what Balaam son of Beor answered... with what shall I come before the Lord and bow down before the exalted God? Shall I come before him with burnt offerings, with calves a year old? Will the Lord be pleased with thousands of rams, with ten thousand rivers of oil? Shall I offer my firstborn for my transgression, the fruit of my body for the sin of my soul?

Balaam, still under the influence of the Holy Spirit answered:

He has showed you oh man, what is good and what does the Lord require of you? To act justly, and to love mercy and to walk humbly with your God. (Micah 6:5-9)

It is unfortunate that neither Balaam nor Balak listened to the inspired counsel. What does the Lord really require? Balaam, by the

Spirit, offers a concise summary of what God requires – righteousness, mercy and humility. He requires nothing less than perfect righteousness. But because of the complete lack thereof, He also requires the reception of His own mercy, which is forgiveness – propitiation by substitution – and the humility which would accompany such a faith. The real God requires righteousness, but what He requires, in mercy, He provides! This should inspire utter humility before Him.

But Balak and Balaam each worshiped their own gods. Balak's god had already proven impotent, unable to stop the Israelite advance, unable to even allow them to be cursed. Balaam's gods were money, prestige and position. He would not defect from them even in the face of the power of the God of Israel!

It would be a long trip home for Balaam; this time he would not be accompanied by the Arab nobles who had crossed the four-hundred-mile desert twice previously to court him. There would be lots of time to think, though. But there would be no reward, no honor nor prestige for him, he had failed to successfully overcome Genesis 12:3, he simply couldn't curse Israel. The God of Israel could not be induced to turn against them.

It was perhaps on this trip home that the inspiration came to him, the idea that rather than cursing Israel, perhaps by luring Israel into gross and abominable sin, she might be induced into bringing the judgment of the Holy God upon herself. This is the doctrine of Balaam that Jesus warned about.

Balak and Balaam met again, apparently, and organized a pagan festival at Baal Peor, that is, "Lord of the Opening," within range of the encamped children of Israel. Paganism was and is a sensual affair – altars to Baal were set up, choice offerings of beef were set upon the grills, sensual music was conducted and the wives, daughters and virgins of Midian and Moab were presented as sacred prostitutes to any and all who were drawn to the party.

And Israel abode in Shittim, and the people began to commit whoredom with the daughters of Moab. And they called the people to the sacrifices of their gods, and the people did eat and bowed down. And Israel joined herself to Baal Peor, and the anger of the LORD was kindled against Israel. (Numbers 25:1-3)

To the ones who left the camp of Israel, following the siren sound of the pagan music, the festival to Baal could be rationalized as just a sensual experience and nothing more. The aroma of the choice steaks cooking on the altars of Baal, the pleasures of the wine and women of Midian were all just a little relief from the monotony of a lifetime in the desert eating manna. We don't really believe in Baal, we just need to blow off a little steam.

But to God, these experiences represented so much more. *"Israel has joined herself to Baal Peor, she has yoked herself to an alien god, she has played the harlot."* So it is today that too often, even a confessing Christian can also rationalize that compromise with fornication, pornography, worldliness and false religion are meaningless, when it isn't. Perhaps a similar soul-killing plague is broken out among us also, and we just don't realize it!

When a plague broke out in the camp of Israel, it almost looked as though Balaam's teaching would obtain the intended result. God had not turned against Israel, but by Balaam's counsel, Israel had turned against God and would now pay the price of judgment against them.

But Moses quickly responded to the divine command to hang the leaders of the defection, thus transferring the curse that had come upon the nation onto the cursed ones hanging on the trees. The swords of the judges of Israel also destroyed the men who had corrupted themselves. Decisive action is required in the face of such defection and apostasy.

But in the midst of such a scene, we encounter another very modern and relevant phenomenon; the blatant gall of evil. Evil has become so bold it is almost paralyzing to those who seek to overcome it. It no longer hides; it has come out into the open and challenges us to our face.

130

And behold, one of the children of Israel came and brought unto his brethren a Midianitish woman in the sight of Moses, and in the sight of all of the congregation of the children of Israel, who were weeping before the door of the tabernacle of the congregation. (Numbers 25:6)

Boldly walking into the camp, "in everyone's face," even while people all around were weeping and repenting at the tabernacle, and others were burying some of the twenty-four thousand who had died of the plague, strode a prince of Israel and a Midianitish princess. The leaders of the apostasy were hanging on trees, but this Israelite had the gall to openly flaunt the sin that had caused such suffering. This is the blatancy of evil and it called for some kind of reaction, for it was a direct challenge to the congregation of Israel.

But Phineas, the grandson of Aaron the High Priest, without hesitation stood up in the congregation and with spear in hand followed the brazen couple to their conjugal tent, where he ran them through with his spear. Thus Israel –through Phineas in his representative capacity as their priest – rejected the idolatry and fornication and the plague was stopped. Balaam had again failed to curse Israel.

But the consequences for listening to Balaam were forthcoming for Balak and his people, and they would be severe. Deuteronomy tells us that because of the doctrine of Balaam, none of the next ten generations of Moabites would be admitted into the congregation of Israel. A war of extermination was commenced against Balak's kingdom.

The utter destruction of this culture of evil, as recorded in Numbers 31, has caused many to accuse the Israelites of genocide – and the God who commanded them of being barbaric. But what kind of culture would be so intent on resisting Genesis 12:3, that it would offer its women and girls as prostitutes in order to destroy Israel? Certainly a death-loving culture for whom marriage is nothing and where there is nothing sacred – nothing could compare with the

131

desire for revenge and destruction.

This part of the story also is eerily relevant to today. The spiritual, moral and, in some cases physical, descendants of the Moabites and Midianites also hate Israel so badly that they are willing to use sex and sexuality to destroy them. In its current manifestation, this involves the promise to miserable, frustrated, unemployed young men the eternal use of 72 perpetual virgins – if they would be willing to commit mass murder of Jews. What do you suppose the future holds for this toxic culture?

Balaam had once prophesied wistfully that he would want to die the death of righteous Israel rather than curse them. But alas for him, he took his stand rather with the wicked and is in hell today, having been found among the corpses of the princes of Midianites. Like Judas, he knew all too well what the truth was, but his inward affinities took him elsewhere.

The nations of the world today face the same choice, to either side with Israel, and perhaps to die the blessed "death of the Righteous," or to take sides with blatant evil, with hatred and revenge, and with those who would see marriage and sexuality as a means to their own murderous end. Like Balaam, too many of the nations of the world have only asked one question: "What's in it for me?" Thus they are falling under the curse of Genesis 12:3 rather than the blessing. They have allowed themselves to side with barbarism against the only civilized country in the region; therefore, they are soon to be filled with their own ways.

Chapter 26 – Israel's Final Conflict and Rescue: A Brief Look at Zechariah 12

This is the word of the LORD concerning Israel. The LORD, who stretches out the heavens, who lays the foundation of the earth, and who forms the spirit of man within him, declares: "I am going to make Jerusalem a cup that sends all the surrounding peoples reeling. Judah will be besieged as well as Jerusalem. On that day, when all the nations of the earth are gathered against her, I will make Jerusalem an immovable rock for all the nations. All who try to move it will injure themselves. (Zechariah 12:1-3)

The last chapters of Zechariah have an amazing relevance to the world situation we see unfolding before us today. I would like to lift a few phrases within the passage to highlight this startling relevance to today.

First of all, notice the signature in the first verse. Who is this oracle coming from? It is uttered in the name of the Creator God, literally the one who continuously sustains his creation, continuously upholding the heavens, and who continuously grants to man his very being! The self-existent sustainer and author of life and being will one day make Jerusalem to become *"a cup of trembling"* (KJV) to those nations round about her.

Secondly, He says "I will make...." In other words, whatever happens in the Middle East, with all of the ugly, painful and trying ramifications of the conflict there, we are to know that it is not the 'Palestinians' or the Muslims, Christians or Jews who have provoked this situation. God Himself says, "I will make ...." for it is HE Himself who has provoked this world-engulfing crisis.

Thirdly, "JERUSALEM." "I *will make JERUSALEM a cup of trembling...."* Consider the significance of Jerusalem:

• The only city on earth of which God has said that He would "put His name there: *"And unto his son will I give one tribe, that David my servant may have a light always before me in Jerusalem, the city which I have chosen me to put my name there."* (I Kings 11:36)

•   Jerusalem is the place where Jesus won for us the victory over sin, death and evil, at Mt. Calvary, and where He arose from the grave. In other words, it is the city where Satan was dealt a fatal blow by the Lord.

•   Jerusalem is the place designated by God for our Lord to return, for Zechariah also tells us, "His foot shall land on the Mt of Olives."

•   Jerusalem is the, "City of the great King," as Psalm 48 tells us, "Great is the Lord, and greatly to be praised in the city of our God, in the
mountain of his holiness."

"...beautiful for situation, the joy of the whole earth, is mount Zion, on the sides of the north, the city of the great King."

Jesus quoted this Psalm in the sermon on the mount when he cautioned against swearing:

"But I say unto you, Swear not at all; neither by heaven; for it is God's throne: Nor by the earth; for it is his footstool: neither by Jerusalem; for it is the city of the great King." (Matthew 5:34-35)

•   The Bible is realistic about Jerusalem, however, calling it, "Sodom and Egypt, the place where our Lord was crucified..." in Revelation 11.

However, consider also the modern significance of the city:

•   Jerusalem is the only city split in two by the U.N.

•   Jerusalem is the only capitol that the nations of the world refuse to place embassies at.

•   Jerusalem is never mentioned in the Koran by name, yet Islam claims it as the "third holiest site" of the Mohammedan religion.

•   The one indirect reference to Jerusalem in the Koran is the "Izra," the story which has Mohammed riding a white winged

134

horse to the "Furthest places" (Al Aqsa), in order to ascend into the heavens for a prayer meeting with Jesus and Moses.

•   When Barak Hussein Obama made an unprecedented address to the Muslim world from Al Azhar University (the Harvard and Cambridge of world Islamic terrorism) at Cairo, he cited one Koranic passage... the Izra, the only reference that would even remotely validate Muslim claims to Jerusalem!

•   When the Democratic National Convention met in the year 2012 to decide upon a platform upon which to run a national campaign, they voted to expunge references to God and to Jerusalem (every year until then, one of the planks was to recognize Jerusalem as the capital of Israel). When senior party officials called for a floor vote to put "God" and "Jerusalem" back into the platform, they were loudly booed on national television.

Fourthly, consider the phrase "a cup of trembling." What is this "cup of trembling"? In scripture, it is a metaphor for a devastating national judgment, one which causes a nation to reel, become confused and disoriented, and eventually to go mad, having lost the capacity for sound judgment, and set on a course of national self-destruction.

In the hand of the LORD is a cup full of foaming wine mixed with spices; he pours it out, and all the wicked of the earth drink it down to its very dregs.
(Psalm 75:8)

Israel herself was made to drink to the dregs this cup, for she went mad in the last days before the destruction of the nation and temple in 70 AD. Everything she did undermined her, factions within tore her asunder, and her leaders were given a self-destructive spirit, until the nation was dissolved and dispersed abroad. But Isaiah tells us that in the last days, God would remove the cup of trembling from Zion and cause the nations who oppress her to drink of it, to their destruction!

Therefore hear this, you
    afflicted one, made drunk,
    but not with wine.

This is what your Sovereign
    Lord says, your God, who
    defends his people:
"See, I have taken out of
    your hand the cup that
    made you stagger;
from that cup, the goblet of
    my wrath, you will never
    drink again.

I will put it into the hands of your
    tormentors, who said to you,
    'Fall prostrate that we may walk
on you.' And you made your back
    like the ground,
    like a street to be walked on." (Isaiah 51:17, 21-23)

True to this prophecy, the nations of the world are presently in great turmoil about the so-called "status" of Jerusalem. Though Jerusalem is manifestly the ancient and well-established capital of the state of Israel, virtually none of the nations of the world will put an embassy there, including the USA. They fear inflaming the Moslem near-neighbors of Israel.

The Obama administration has attempted to make the appeasement of the Muslim world a centerpiece of its foreign policy. Therefore, it has taken an unprecedented US stance toward Israel, especially regarding Jerusalem and Judea.

Islam has been claiming that Jerusalem has never been anything but a Muslim city, one of the "holiest" sites of the Muslim faith. Yet the Koran doesn't mention Jerusalem by name anywhere.

In its effort to erase any sign of Jewish history in Jerusalem, the Wafq, the Muslim custodianship of the Temple Mount, has been moving tons of rubble from beneath the surface of the site of the temple, dumping it in gravel pits outside of the city. Archeologists are finding priceless artifacts of the previous two temples in the rubble.

There is a reference in the Koran to "Al Aqsa," literally, the "farthest place" from Mecca, where Mohammed supposedly rode a winged horse *en route* to a heavenly Muslim prayer meeting with Jesus and Moses. It is interesting that in Obama's Cairo speech to the Muslim world, he referenced this obscure story, "the Isra," the sole Muslim claim to Jerusalem, and that only by inference.

The Bible, however, has more than 800 direct references to Jerusalem. It is "the city of the great King," the "Joy of the whole earth," Mt. Zion, the sight of the future capital of the world, the counterpart to "the heavenly Jerusalem." God is "zealous for Jerusalem with a great fury," we are told earlier in Zechariah.

Jerusalem, we are told by our Lord Jesus, will be trodden under foot of the Gentiles until the time of the Gentiles be fulfilled. For the time being, it is as "Sodom and Egypt" (Revelation 11) but is destined to be the city where righteousness dwells, and out of which the Law of the Lord shall stream forth to all of the world. No wonder there is such a storm around it.

Jerusalem is the only city on earth of which it could be said that God has placed his name there! It is the center of the earth, and the Temple Mount (Zion) is the center of Jerusalem. Psalm 48 tells us it is "the city of the great King." Jesus quoted that verse in the sermon on the mount, saying, "Swear not at all by Jerusalem, for it is the city of the great King!"

The U.N. wants to make it an international city, the Vatican wants custodianship over it, Islam claims it as one of its holiest sites. The Gentiles insist on it being divided into two cities: one the capital of the "Palestinian" state, the other side the capital of the Jewish state. Islam doesn't like the name Jerusalem, they call it "Al Quds", and so did a senior Obama security advisor in a speech recently.

There is a storm brewing exactly as the prophet said it would; God is making Jerusalem a cup of trembling, making mad the nations of the world.

Another phrase, "When they shall be in siege, against Jerusalem and Judah"... On the world scene, Jerusalem and Judea are two different issues, much discussed and argued over. Judea is the very heart of biblical Israel, the "mountains of Israel," but which has been designated by the U.N. and the nations as part of the "Palestinian Authority." It is never referred to as Judea in the world press; rather it is either called "The West Bank," the "Occupied territory" or "Palestine." But God calls it Judea and has dedicated an entire chapter in Ezekiel to it, Ezekiel 36.

Jesus, in the quintessential chapter on prophecy from the gospels, Matthew 24, Jesus speaks in universal terms at first, warning of earthquakes, wars, famines and deceivers coming in his name. But all of the sudden Jesus waxes local and regional when he warns, "Then let them who are Judea flee." Something happens that will necessitate flight at the outbreak of the "great tribulation." The world condemns the Jewish settlers of Judea as being obstacles to peace.

Obama and his secretary of state have called for a strict "no natural growth" policy for Judea (the West Bank), and they have severely condemned Israel for approving the building of housing units in East Jerusalem.

In the amazing prediction of Zechariah 12:1-2, we are told that, in the last days, Jerusalem would become a point of international contention, ultimately drawing the whole world into the strife. The text goes on further to predict:

"And it shall happen in that day that I will make Jerusalem a very heavy stone for all peoples; all who would heave it away will surely be cut to pieces, though all nations of the earth be gathered against it." (Zechariah 12:3)

Then God says that it is He that will make Jerusalem to be a stone that "the nations of the earth" would presume to pick up and carry away; however, they would find to their detriment that it is too heavy for them to do so. The ones who try are literally "lacerated" for their failed efforts.

The idea is that in some way, "all of the nations of the earth" are walking down a road, progressing towards a common goal, a godless technocratic utopia! But they come to an obstruction in the road, a heavy stone that sits in the way of progress. Jerusalem is that stone; it's (Jewish) status trips up the oil-rich Muslim nations that the West depends upon for the continuance of the New World Order they are seeking to erect. The continuance of Israel as a sovereign nation, and Jerusalem as her capitol, is an affront to the Muslim world.

The United Nations must do something about it. Only recently, with the emergence of the U.N., has the prophecy, "all of the nations of the earth," been viable. For the first time, all nations of the earth are in a congress with regular meetings.

The road is the path towards some kind of globalist "world order." It is post-national, post-Christian, the possible fulfillment of the utopian ideals of millions over the centuries. The day is almost here; it is right around the corner. "Peace on earth and goodwill towards men" (of course without God). But there is one stubborn trouble spot: the Middle East! How are we going to solve the quarrel between Jacob and Esau?

It doesn't matter who; every one of the "Kings of the earth and their rulers," who have tried to solve the problem of the so-called status of Jerusalem, have failed, to their own hurt. The sun set on the British Empire because of it.

Uncle Sam says, "I'll take care of it," and rolls up his sleeves and squats to lift the stone but cannot move it, and has severe cuts on his arms to show for his efforts. Every American president since Eisenhower has tried and failed to solve the Jerusalem problem. None of them would dare move the US Embassy to it out of deference to the Muslims, although most of them promised to when running for office.

In the first year of his administration, President Obama made an unprecedented appeal to the Muslim world, and that from Cairo, Egypt. He made clear in the speech his sympathy with Muslims and his desire for the so-called "two-state" solution to be imposed upon the land God gave to Abraham, Isaac and Jacob.

Obama personally has condemned the Netanyahu government for authorizing the building of housing in East Jerusalem. His administration, as well as the U.N., the EU and Russia, believe that East Jerusalem should be reserved as the capital of the Palestinian state.

Ominously, one of Obama's national security advisors, John Brennon, recently referred to Jerusalem as "Al Quds" in a speech to an Arab-American student group. "Al Quds" is the name given to Jerusalem by Islamists who want to deny the Jewish history of the city, insisting that it has always been Muslim and never Jewish.

This pandering to Islamic terrorists by a representative of the world's lone superpower is an example of just how heavy the stone is and how desperate the world is to move it.

Zechariah's prophecy comes closer to realization as the "status" of Jerusalem is argued about and maneuvered by the movers and shakers of the world. I just dread the "lacerations" that are sure to follow. Maranatha Lord Jesus!

"In that day says the Lord, I will strike every horse with **confusion**, *and its rider with* **madness***; I will open my eyes on the house of Judah, and will strike every horse of the peoples with* **blindness***... In that day I will make the governors of Judah like a firepan in the woodpile, and like a fiery torch in the sheaves; they shall devour all the surrounding peoples on the right hand and on the left, but Jerusalem shall be inhabited again in her own place-Jerusalem."* (Zechariah 12:4-6)

What will be the outcome of Jerusalem being made a "cup of trembling," maddening her near neighbors into an irrational, self-destructive fury? How will the world eventually react to the "burdensome stone," which frustrates the nations of the world in their quest for a godless Utopia? Her enemies, near and far, will rise up against her in a series of brief and intense wars, in which they will ultimately be utterly defeated.

Zechariah 12:2 already predicted that the nations around her would be "in siege" against her. In June 2010, the news was dominated by the "flotilla fiasco," which seems to underscore this fact. Ultimately, the Arab Muslim neighbors of Israel – Arabia, Yemen, southern Lebanon (Hezbullah), Gaza (Hamas), Jordan, Syria and Iraq – will unite in a concerted effort to see to it "that the name of Israel be remembered no more" (Psalm 83:4), as the 83rd Psalm predicts.

Ezekiel 38 also predicts a coming war against Israel, this time from the rest of the Muslim world, yet headed up by Russia, Libya, Ethiopia, Somalia, Turkey, and the Turkik republics of the Caucasian mountains; all will descend as a cloud to "take a spoil," but the devastation will almost be absolute!

In the quote above, I have highlighted in bold the three words of the curse that God will put on the adversaries: confusion, blindness and madness. The cup God makes the nations of the world to drink will cause them to be confused; it will blind them, and it will make them utterly mad!

The ironic thing is that this is the same cup God caused Israel to drink when He judged her. According to the curse of the Law, in Deuteronomy 28:28-29:

"The Lord will strike you with blindness, madness and confusion of heart, and you shall grope at noonday, as a blind man gropes in darkness; you shall not prosper in your ways; you will only be oppressed and plundered continually and no one will save you."

Now that the set time to favor Israel has come, the cup she once had to drink is to be given to those Gentile nations that have oppressed her and furthered her afflictions all these years. This is the meaning of the utter madness of the Arab nations for the last sixty years, as well as the madness that is now afflicting the rest of the world's leaders.

Just two maxims will suffice to illustrate such blind, confused madness. "The Palestinians never miss an opportunity to miss an opportunity"–by an Israeli politician (I am not sure which one). And this by Golda Meir, "Peace will not come to the Middle East until the Muslims decide that they will love their own children more than they hate us." Does this not illustrate the self-defeating, retrograde, consistently destructive policy that the Arab Muslim world has pursued these many years?

And now this cup of madness is being indulged in by Obama, the European Union, the Russians and the rest of the so-called "Kings of the Earth and their rulers" (Psalm 2). There can be no other explanation for the contrary, self-destructive, ruinous policies our "intelligentsia" are pursuing.

Abortion? Madness! Homosexual marriage? Utter madness! Global warming and the policies that will affect millions and will ruin otherwise modern, thriving economies? Insanity! It seems that common sense has died, and the leaders of the world can't make a sound decision. As God says in Proverbs 8 of His Wisdom, "All they that hate me, love death!"

We are at the stage in world history that Isaiah prophesied:

"Therefore hear this you afflicted, and drunk but not with wine. Thus says the Lord, the LORD your God, who pleads the cause of His people, see I have taken out of your hand the cup of trembling, the dregs of the cup of my fury; you shall no longer drink it, But I will put it into the hand of those who afflict you, Who have said unto you, 'Lie down that we may walk over you...'" (Isaiah 51:21-23)

"In that day I will make Jerusalem a burdensome stone for all the peoples to lift, all who lift it shall injure themselves" (Zechariah 12:2)

The word for "injure themselves" can be interpreted as "lacerate themselves."

On the very week that the Ariel Sharon administration succumbed to the long years of American diplomatic pressure on

Israel to evacuate Gush Katif, the Jewish community in Gaza, hurricane Katrina struck our southern coastal area, ultimately to the detriment of the Bush presidency.

The following bullet points are from a *World Net Daily* article about the Gaza/Katrina connection.

• Gaza's Jewish communities were located in Israel's southern coastal region; America's southern coastal region now lies in ruins.

• The U.S. government called on Louisiana residents to evacuate their homes ahead of the storm. The Israeli government, backed by statements from U.S. officials, demanded Gaza residents evacuate their homes.

• Katrina, written in Hebrew, has a numerical equivalent of 374, according to a biblical numbering system upheld by all traditional Jewish authorities. Two relevant passages in the Torah share the exact numerical equivalent: "They have done you evil" (Gen. 50:17), and "The sea upon land" (Exodus 14:15).

• Bush, from Texas, and Rice, from Alabama, were the most vocal U.S. backers of the Gaza evacuation. Hurricane Katrina hit the states in between Texas and Alabama: Louisiana and Mississippi.

• Similarity in scenes: Many residents of Jewish Gaza climbed to their rooftops to escape the threat of expulsion, while residents of the Gulf Coast climbed on their own rooftops to protect themselves from the rising waters. Jewish Gaza homes described as beautiful and charming were demolished this week by Israel's military. Once beautiful homes in New Orleans now lie in ruins.

• The day Katrina hit, Israel began carrying out what was termed the most controversial aspect of the Gaza withdrawal: the uprooting of bodies from the area's Jewish cemetery. There have been media reports of corpses
floating around in flooded New Orleans regions.

• *Did God Send Katrina as a Judgment for Gaza?*
by Aaron Klein http://www.wnd.com/?pageId=32196

Now fast forward to April 19th, 2010, which happened to be the 62nd anniversary of the modern state of Israel. While millions of Jews and friends of Israel celebrated the fulfillment of the prophecies of Israel's regathering and rebirth, President Obama gave a speech outlining changes in foreign policy, most notably towards Israel. The changes involved the longstanding use by the United States of veto power in the U.N. Security Council whenever anti-Israel resolutions are introduced.

I quote from an April 19th, 2010 FoxNews.com article entitled; "Obama and Israel; Showdown at the UN?" by Ben Evansky :

> The Obama administration is reportedly signaling another major shift in policy towards one of its staunchest allies, Israel, and this shift could change the way it votes at the Security Council. The change would mean an end to the US' use of its veto power in the United Nations Security Council when certain anti-Israel resolutions are introduced for a vote.
>
> Reports surfaced a couple of weeks ago, that a senior US diplomat met with Qatar's foreign minister in Paris. They discussed the possibility that the US was giving serious consideration to not using its veto if a vote on Israeli settlements was to come up. It has been the policy of successive administrations to veto virtually all anti-Israel resolutions at the Security
> Council....

The very next day, April 20th, 2010, an explosion on a Gulf of Mexico oil rig killed eleven workers and commenced the world's worst natural disaster, which has not even yet been abated!

Chapter 27 — The Climax of World History

"I will pour out on the house of David and on the inhabitants of Jerusalem, the Spirit of grace and of supplication, so that they will look on Me whom they have pierced; and they will mourn for Him, as one mourns for an only son, and they will weep bitterly over Him like the bitter weeping over a firstborn." (Zechariah 12:10 NASB)

All of the prophecies of the end times presuppose Israel back in her own land, besieged by the nations of the world. The hatred of this world for God will be vented upon the people whom God made for himself, and who spurned and turned away from him. The last thing Jesus said to Israel in his official capacity as Messiah was, "You shall not see me again until you cry 'blessed is He who comes in the name of the Lord!'"

O Jerusalem, Jerusalem, thou that killest the prophets, and stonest them which are sent unto thee, how often would I have gathered thy children together, even as a hen gathereth her chickens under her wings, and ye would not! Behold, your house is left unto you desolate. For I say unto you, Ye shall not see me henceforth, till ye shall say, Blessed is he that cometh in the name of the Lord. (Matthew 23:27-39)

What will it take to bring the reconstituted, secular nation of Israel to the point where they recognize Jesus and call out to Him as their Messiah? Nothing less than a long night of tribulation, a "time of Jacob's trouble," a repudiation by all nations!

All of the pressures being brought to bear on Israel will lead to that end. Her rejection by the world community, the unrelenting hatred of the Arab/Muslim world, the fact that the Arabs have been put in a position of power by the placement of easy, high-grade crude oil, the rise of anti-Semitism in Europe and elsewhere: all are calculated by Satan to destroy Israel, but they are being used by God to get her to the point of desperation in which she will call out to

God for salvation.

Israel's back will be against the wall; the siege will seem to work, as the Kings of the earth converge upon her to finally wipe her out. At that point, Zechariah predicts that her God shall arise to come to her defense,

Behold, the day of the Lord cometh, and thy spoil shall be divided in the midst of thee.

For I will gather all nations against Jerusalem to battle; and the city shall be taken, and the houses rifled, and the women ravished; and half of the city shall go forth into captivity, and the residue of the people shall not be cut off from the city. Then shall the Lord go forth, and fight against those nations, as when he fought in the day of battle. And his feet shall stand in that day upon the mount of Olives... (Zechariah 14:1-3)

Zechariah says that in the midst of this final end-times siege, Israel will be given the spirit of grace and supplication, an anointing of Godly sorrow for sin and unbelief. They will have to experience a real day of atonement, a deep soul-searching, and at that point, *"They will look upon Me whom they have pierced...."*

When did you pierce the LORD, Israel?

"They will mourn for Him as for an only son and they shall weep over him bitterly as one that weepeth for an only Son..."

The weeping will be both national and corporate, as well as individual. The mourning will involve every person, "In that day there will be great mourning in Jerusalem... every family by itself and their wives by themselves," at the recognition of the enormity of the national sin against the heavenly antitype of Joseph.

That this is the One Isaiah and David predicted; despised and rejected, and pierced for our sins, will be manifest to all of the nation. This risen Christ, who arrested the Pharisee, will arrest the Pharisee nation, in their deepest national crisis. He will come to them and reveal His redeeming wounds to them.

We are told that on that day, a fountain shall open to them for cleansing of sin. Of this fountain the church has long been familiar

146

and cherished ,for we testify of it often, even in songs such as,

> There is a fountain filled
> with blood, Drawn from
> Emmanuel's veins
> And sinners plunged beneath
> the flood, Lose all their
> guilty stains.

Another effect of the opening to Israel of this cleansing fountain is that the same shall finally quench the spirit of false prophecy which has bedeviled and deceived Israel these many centuries.

Appendix 1

God Indicts the Nations: Joel 3

For, behold, in those days, and in that time, when I shall bring again the captivity of Judah and Jerusalem, I will also gather all nations, and will bring them down into the valley of Jehoshaphat, and will plead with them there for my people and for my heritage Israel, whom they have scattered among the nations, and parted my land. And they have cast lots for my people; and have given a boy for an harlot, and sold a girl for wine, that they might drink. (Joel 3:1-3)

At a breathtaking rate, the prophecies of scripture are being fulfilled in geopolitical events occurring right before our eyes. Nations are lining up exactly as foretold in the predictions of Isaiah, Jeremiah, Ezekiel, Zechariah, Joel and the rest of the Hebrew prophets, and behaving as we were told they would in the last days of human history.

This segment of Joel chapter three is an incredible example of this phenomenon.

First of all, Joel sets the time for the prophecy to be fulfilled "In those days and at that time, when I (the LORD) return again the captivity of Judah and Jerusalem." This is something only possible of fulfillment since May 1948, for it was on that date that the nation of Israel was reborn after her long exile among the various gentile nations for centuries. This also was exactly what the prophets had predicted.

It is an amazing sign to the world that since 1948, from all over the world the descendants of Abraham, Isaac and Jacob have been making aliyah, returning to the Promised Land. The modern Exodus has involved Jews scattered as widely as India, China, Russia, Africa and even Mongolia, responding to the call to return to the land of Israel, as God proclaimed they would.

Hear the word of the LORD, O nations,
  And declare it in the isles afar
off, and say, 'He who scattered
Israel will gather him,
  And keep him as a shepherd does his flock.' (Jeremiah
  31:10)

Then the LORD will put the nations under indictment. This is the meaning of the phrase, "I will plead with them there." God isn't pleading with the nations here as we understand pleading; this is legal language: He is filing charges, making a case, and indeed He is bringing the nations unto the seat of judgment.

The name of the valley, "Jehoshaphat," makes this point, for it means, "The LORD shall judge."

The issue will be the treatment of His people, Israel, and though the international consensus is increasingly anti-Israel, the God of the universe is still pro-Israel. God loves his people and won't let them go! He made a promise to Abraham and to his seed, "I will bless those who bless you and curse those who curse you."

Yes indeed God has chastened his people, being a "little displeased " with them, but the nations of the world have taken the chastisement further than the LORD intended, so now He is "sore displeased with the nations."

Thus saith the LORD of hosts; I am jealous for Jerusalem and for Zion with a great jealousy. And I am very sore displeased with the heathen that are at ease: for I was but a little displeased (with Israel), *and they* (the nations) *helped forward the affliction.* (Zechariah 1:14-15)

The four indictments are as follows:

*   Count 1, *"they scattered my people among the nations."* Divine judgment is coming upon the world for the centuries of anti-Semitic persecution, ranging from the ancient nations all the way up to the modern era and the harsh treatment the nations have dealt to God's chosen people. Europe and America are not innocent in this

regard, obviously neither is the Arab world, nor the orient.

- Count Two, *"They have parted my Land."* The nations of the world are seeking to partition and dole out the land that God gave to Abraham, Isaac and Jacob. Whether they are constantly pressuring Israel to cede "land for peace" or to push them back into the indefensible "pre-1967 borders," the "kings of the World and their rulers" are trying to part the land.

About a third of the debate in the U.N. is devoted to this issue of the land: how to divide it to make room for a "two-state solution." Various political leaders, as well as religious, media and other leaders, use their influence to de-legitimize Israel and her right to exist in the land God gave her fathers.

Even Israeli leaders would give up the land if they could, for they, for the most part, don't make scripture as their claim to the land. But they can't ever truly give up the land, for it is not even theirs to dispose of as they see fit.

The land must not be sold permanently, because the land is mine and you reside in my land as foreigners and strangers. (Leviticus 25:23)

- Count 3 is that, *"They have cast lots for my people."*

Only recently has it even been conceivable, let alone possible, for the nations of the world to meet in a congress and literally "cast lots" over the status, fate and disposition of God's people, Israel. The U.N. was founded a few months before the establishment of the modern state of Israel. It is in that forum that the nations of the world meet and cast countless votes regarding the status of Jerusalem, the boundaries of Israel, the legitimacy of its claims, and votes to approve or disapprove the validity of the complaints of her malicious neighbors.

Here is an excerpt from an *EretzYisrael.org* report, the United Nation's record *vis-a-vis* Israel:

"Prior to the Madrid Conference of '91, the office of Prime Minister Yitzhak Shamir commissioned Shai Ben-Tekoa to do a statistical analysis of U.N. voting *vis-a-vis* Israel. The following is a summary of Mr. Ben-Tekoa's research.

Summary

Security Council:

- 175 Total Resolutions
- 74 Neutral
- 4 Against the perceived interests of an Arab state or body
- 97 Against Israel General Assembly:
- Cumulative Number of Votes cast with/for Israel: 7,938.
- Cumulative Number of Votes cast against Israel: 55,642 (From EretzIsrael.org)

- Count Four is that the nations of the world have prostituted their own values, selling out Israel's children to appease Muslim nations so that the supply of oil will flow. One example is the Obama administration's "no growth" policy for Judea, which caps the number of Jews who can live in the heart of Biblical Israel, Judea. As one Obama Middle East adviser stated, "This means if a Jewish baby is born in the morning, an older Jewish person will have to leave by sundown."

They sold a boy for a harlot, and a girl for wine. What is a harlot? Isn't it one for whom all is for sale for the cause of immediate gratification, where even scruples and principles are exchanged?

The West in particular has sold its vaunted values of human rights and rule by law, selling out the Jewish people in order to appease the Muslim world (the world's greatest abusers of human rights) to insure ready access to cheap crude oil. This is the wine that the world sells the only true democracy and civilized country in the Middle East for.

The infinitely Holy and righteous judge of the earth sees all of this.

Appendix 2

Of False Love and Knee-Jerk Reactions...

The world cannot hate you; but me it hateth, because I testify of it, that the works thereof are evil. (John 7:7)

If the world hate you, ye know that it hated me before it hated you. If ye were of the world, the world would love his own: but because ye are not of the world, but I have chosen you out of the world, therefore the world hateth you.
(John 15:18-19)

Increasingly over the past couple of years, many of us within evangelical Christianity have either been a participant in or an observer of the following kind of several-step exchange:

Step 1) A Christian "celebrity" proposes that the church needs to be more tolerant of homosexuality.

Step 2) A Christian disciple takes an exception to it and reaffirms the biblical position on homosexuality.

Step 3) Another Christian disciple, no doubt equally sincere, takes the brother in step 2 to task for asserting the biblical position on the subject. He (or she) usually demands, "Where is the grace?" or some variation of ,"Why do you have to be so harsh and unloving?" or "How are we going to reach these injured souls if all we do is judge them like that?"

Step 4) The Christian concerned about upholding and affirming the biblical view of marriage, sex and gender, is put on the defensive, as though to do so is unloving. He is made to justify himself that he is indeed loving to sinners.

Step 5) The next step is usually the assertion of a moral equivalence between homosexuality and gluttony, lies or being critical. (By then, the "Pharisee" word has been brandished, either openly or implicitly, and in some cases, the "hypocrite" word.)

Step 6) As the discussion progresses, usually the entire

believing church is castigated for being harsh and unloving (for the last 19 centuries), casting out people when they should have been including them and winning them over in love!

How did we arrive at this place? What is this that has come to divide the last bastion of resistance to the agenda of those who would annihilate all of the God-ordained distinctions, including male and female?

I believe I have a theory that can explain this.

Mind you, my theory only addresses the church side of this multifaceted problem. There are other factors that feed into this schism as well, which would be good topics for another time. What I believe has happened is that there are a good many pastors who are worldly and misunderstand and shun the reproach of Christ. They don't get that it is at just that point that the world is currently rebelling against God, that the church must bear humble witness to the Truth, even if it exposes the church to hatred, reproach and abuse. We are not always going to be loved and appreciated.

These pastors have been trained humanistically; they think in terms of man: they have a man-centered gospel and are unfamiliar with concepts such as the holiness of God or the centrality of the glory of God. They are very much in tune with, and good at tapping into, the "Spirit of the Age," and then to Christianize it. A good many of them are hip youth group leader types, only grown older.

The current "Spirit of the Age" is tolerance and acceptance, even of the unacceptable, and non-judgmentalism. Everything is the Civil Rights movement of the sixties, and no one wants to be the next Bull Connor. This is the current delusion.

What these pastors are more than willing to do is to criticize the church (and I mean the whole church down through the ages) as having been unloving, uncaring and judgmental to people who need it the most. They do this so they can contrast themselves and their own ilk as being the only compassionate and humane ones. This is posturing, and it is effective. They get to be Jesus, whilst the vast majority of the church get to be the Pharisees. Especially those who

153

dare speak out, asserting biblical truth with any kind of authority, as authority is taboo now; we are all supposed to be conflicted and uncertain, even apologetic!

I have seen this played out many times. I have seen pastors actually apologize on behalf of the church (not their own church mind you) to the "homosexual community" for years of alleged maltreatment by Christians. This is the false love: it is humanistic, misguided, and is seducing a good many to succumb to evil, siding with it in the face of truth, light and goodness.

They actually resist truth in the name of the "love!" The knee-jerk reactions that we see coming from their followers are always against any Christian who dares to assert the biblical position. It is never against those who would distort it or ignore it altogether.

It is also based on a wrong notion of sinners, that they are poor, misunderstood souls who just need someone to uncritically walk alongside of them, as Jesus supposedly did. It doesn't see sinners as the rebels they really are, who would unseat God himself if possible, and who seek to profane everything holy, including and especially the church.

Should the church welcome all sinners regardless of their sins? **Absolutely!** That is a given and it always has been through the centuries, regardless of the accounts of the new compassionate preachers. But should the church accommodate itself to the "gay community?" Should it apologize as though preaching the truth about God's righteousness were wrong or insensitive? Need I even answer this?

I saw an example of this one night watching Larry King. Larry had three guests on. The first was a back-slidden gospel music star, a confused young woman who came out as a lesbian, and was insisting that she could still be a Christian minister.

The second guest was a real Christian, a pastor (I don't even know his name) who spoke lovingly to the young woman. He told her that she could be forgiven of her sin, but needed to repent, and that Jesus could restore her. He insisted that her lesbianism was a sin, but that she could overcome it through Jesus.

The third guest was once the head of the National Association of Evangelicals, and a well known pastor. He interrupted the other pastor with this, saying, "Wait a minute brother, just remember that the only people Jesus ever rebuked were the self-righteous ones who judged others."

Larry King was overjoyed at this "open-minded" preacher! Finally, an evangelical who "gets it!" The young woman was encouraged and bolstered by that response also, so much so that she was able to laugh in the face of the true preacher and ignore his pleadings.

I believe it was the Holy Spirit who spoke to me when I saw that spectacle saying, "Do you see what he just did? He just gained the world!"

He didn't get rich or famous, but for that brief moment, at the very point that the Spirit of the Age was contesting, he was willing to posture, to cut off the truth, so that he could be seen by the world as "one of the good, non-judgmental Christians." At the expense of his loving and truth-telling brother, he gained the world.

This is part of what is behind the schism coming to the believing church. Refusal to share in the reproach of the witness of Christ, the desire to be seen as "loving" by worldly standards, as understanding, compassionate even "with it." They actually resist truth, showing willingness to rebuke those who seriously witness against this generation at their deepest sin and error. May God help us through this trial! May God revive the church!

About the Author
Pastor Bill Randles

I am 51 years old and have served *Believers in Grace Fellowship* since 1982. A non-denominational, Pentecostal church in Marion, Iowa. My wife and I started this church in our living room.

My wife's name is Kristin, and she has given me six awesome children: two daughters, Dara, and Anna, and four sons, Samuel, Marcus, Ian and Ezra. My daughters are married and Dara, our eldest, has seven children, and Anna has three. (My secret plan to take over the world... shhhhhh!)

I have written four books, three of which are critiques of certain heretical trends within Pentecostalism.

1. *MAKING WAR IN THE HEAVENLIES* addresses the spiritual warfare error which emerged in the late eighties and early nineties.

2. *WEIGHED AND FOUND WANTING* puts the so called Toronto blessing in its true context, as a development of the Manifested Sons of God heresy, once denounced by the Assemblies of God, but now embraced.

3. *BEWARE THE NEW PROPHETS* takes on the prophetic movement of Rick Joyner, Mike Bickle, Bob Jones, and Kim Clement, among others.

4. My last book, *MENDING THE NETS,* is a commentary on the First Epistle of John.

Our church has a website which features a lot of my articles and, in audio and video, many of my sermons.

www.believersingrace.com

CPSIA information can be obtained at www.ICGtesting.com
Printed in the USA
BVOW012144120713

325392BV00004B/39/P